JUN   2007

W9-ASL-750

Wind

Other books in the Fueling the Future series:

Biomass: Energy from Plants and Animals
Coal
Geothermal Power
Hydrogen
Natural Gas
Nuclear Power
Oil
Solar Power
Water

Wind

Clay Farris Naff, *Book Editor*

Chris Nasso, *Publisher*
Elizabeth Des Chenes, *Managing Editor*

GREENHAVEN PRESS

An imprint of Thomson Gale, a part of The Thomson Corporation

Detroit • New York • San Francisco • San Diego • New Haven, Conn. • Waterville, Maine • London • Munich

LIBRARY OF CONGRESS CATALOGING-IN-PUBLICATION DATA

Wind / Clay Farris Naff, book editor.
   p. cm. — (Fueling the future)
  Includes bibliographical references and index.
 ISBN 0-7377-3580-5 (hardcover : alk. paper)
  1. Wind power—Juvenile literature. I. Naff, Clay Farris.
 TJ820.W498 2006
 333.9'2—dc22

                                    2006019551

Printed in the United States of America

Contents

Foreword   8

Introduction   10

Chapter 1: The Development of Wind Power

1. **Ancient Sails Harness the Wind**   20
   Leo Block

   The first known use of wind power was to move ancient
   boats along the River Nile in ancient Egypt, starting
   about 6000 B.C.

2. **How Windmills Helped the Dutch Reclaim the**   24
   Netherlands
   Suzanne Beedell

   No country is more reliant on windmills for its existence
   than the Netherlands. Starting in the fifteenth century,
   the Dutch used windmills to pump water out of low-lying
   areas in order to reclaim the land.

3. **How Windmills Helped Pioneers Settle the**   33
   American Southwest
   T. Lindsay Baker

   Pioneers in Texas used wind power to pump underground
   water for crops and cattle, making it possible to settle the
   semiarid land.

Chapter 2: Does Wind Power Benefit the Environment?

1. **Wind Turbines Kill Too Many Birds**   45
   Andrew Chapman

   An engineer specializing in environmental issues
   contends that the whirling blades of wind turbines
   have killed thousands of raptors.

2. **Wind Turbines Kill Relatively Few Birds**   52
   Mick Sagrillo

   A wind energy operator argues that wind turbines cause
   few avian deaths compared with other threats to bird
   safety.

3. **A Cape Cod Wind Farm Would Harm the**   63
   Environment
   Robert F. Kennedy Jr.

   Building a wind farm in Nantucket Sound would harm
   marine wildlife, damage local tourism and fishing
   industries, and mar the beautiful views.

4. **A Cape Cod Wind Farm Would Benefit the**   69
   Environment
   Cape Wind

   The electricity produced by a Cape Cod wind farm
   would reduce America's use of polluting fossil
   fuels, which contribute to global warming.

Chapter 3: Can Wind Energy Fuel the Future?

1. **Wind Energy Can Meet America's Future**   79
   Energy Needs
   John Dunlop and Mike Sloan, interviewed by Ira Flatow

   Two wind energy experts argue that wind energy will
   meet a significant portion of the nation's energy
   needs in the future.

2. **Wind Energy Is Too Expensive**   89
   Neil Hrab

   The use of wind energy to generate electricity is
   prohibitively expensive. In fact, the wind power
   industry would not exist without government
   subsidies.

3. Wind Will Become the World's Leading Energy   95
   Source

   Lester R. Brown

   As new, more efficient turbines become available and
   the cost of fossil fuels climbs, wind energy will become
   the world's primary source of power.

4. Wind Power May Drive the Hydrogen Fuel   102
   Revolution

   Dawn Levy

   Wind power could be harnessed to produce hydrogen,
   which in turn can be used as a clean-burning
   automotive fuel.

Facts About Wind   111

Glossary   113

Chronology   116

For Further Reading   119

Index   123

Picture Credits   127

About the Editor   128

Foreword

The wind farm at Altamont Pass in Northern California epitomizes many people's idea of wind power: Hundreds of towering white turbines generate electricity to power homes, factories, and businesses. The spinning turbine blades call up visions of a brighter future in which clean, renewable energy sources replace dwindling and polluting fossil fuels. The blades also kill over a thousand birds of prey each year. Every energy source, it seems, has its price.

The bird deaths at Altamont Pass make clear an unfortunate fact about all energy sources, including renewables: They have downsides. People want clean, abundant energy to power their modern lifestyles, but few want to pay the costs associated with energy production and use. Oil, coal, and natural gas contain high amounts of energy, but using them produces pollution. Commercial solar energy facilities require hundreds of acres of land and thus must be located in rural areas. Expensive and ugly transmission lines must then be run from the solar plants to the cities that need power. Producing hydrogen for fuel involves the use of dirty fossil fuels, tapping geothermal energy depletes ground water, and growing biomass for fuel ties up land that could be used to grow food. Hydroelectric power has become increasingly unpopular because dams flood vital habitats and kill wildlife and plants. Perhaps most controversial, nuclear power plants produce highly dangerous radioactive waste. People's reluctance to pay these environmental costs can be seen in the results of a 2006 Center for Economic and Civic Opinion poll. When asked how much they would support a power plant in their neighborhood, 66 percent of respondents said they would oppose it.

Many scientists warn that fossil fuel use creates emissions that threaten human health and cause global warming. Moreover, numerous scientists claim that fossil fuels are running out. As a result of these concerns, many nations have begun to revisit the energy sources that first powered human enterprises. In his 2006 State of the Union speech, U.S. President George W. Bush announced that since 2001 the United States has spent "$10 billion to develop cleaner, cheaper, and more reliable alternative energy sources," such as biomass and wind power. Despite Bush's positive rhetoric, many critics contend that the renewable energy sources he refers to are still as inefficient as they ever were and cannot possibly power modern economies. As Jerry Taylor and Peter Van Doren of the Cato Institute note, "The market share for non-hydro renewable energy . . . has languished between 1 and 3 percent for decades." Controversies such as this have been a constant throughout the history of humanity's search for the perfect energy source.

Greenhaven Press's Fueling the Future series explores this history. Each volume in the series traces the development of one energy source, and investigates the controversies surrounding its environmental impact and its potential to power humanity's future. The anthologies provide a variety of selections written by scientists, environmental activists, industry leaders, and government experts. Volumes also contain useful research tools, including an introductory essay providing important context, and an annotated table of contents that enables students to locate selections of interest easily. In addition, each volume includes an index, chronology, bibliography, glossary, and a Facts About section, which lists useful information about each energy source. Other features include numerous charts, graphs, and cartoons, which offer additional avenues for learning important information about the topic.

Fueling the Future volumes provide students with important resources for learning about the energy sources upon which human societies depend. Although it is easy to take energy for granted in developed nations, this series emphasizes how energy sources are also problematic. The U.S. Energy Information Administration calls energy "essential to life." Whether scientists will be able to develop the energy sources necessary to sustain modern life is the vital question explored in Greenhaven Press's Fueling the Future series.

Introduction

In his State of the Union speech, delivered in January 2006, President George W. Bush announced the Advanced Energy Initiative (AEI), which calls on the U.S. Department of Energy to accelerate the development of clean energy sources to power homes, offices, and vehicles. In his speech Bush claimed that the initiative "will help [America] . . . replace more than 75 percent of our oil imports from the Middle East by 2025."[1] Bush's announcement highlights the urgency felt by many American lawmakers and energy experts to transition from a fossil fuels–based economy to one powered by renewable energy sources such as wind.

Many energy experts predict that world oil production will have peaked sometime between 2005 and 2020. After that, they say, production will decline and eventually end as oil runs out. Meanwhile, they say, reliance on imported oil makes America vulnerable to shortages arising from political unrest in petroleum-exporting nations. Other experts maintain that the burning of fossil fuels accelerates global warming through the release of greenhouse gases. These concerns have led to calls for greater investment in renewable energy sources. Much of the attention has focused on wind energy. As the U.S. Department of Energy observes, "Wind energy doesn't pollute the air like power plants that rely on combustion of fossil fuels, such as coal or natural gas. Wind turbines don't produce atmospheric emissions that cause acid rain or greenhouse gasses. . . . Wind energy relies on the renewable power of the wind, which can't be used up."[2] Environmental economist Lester R. Brown remarks that wind is "cheap, abundant, inexhaustible, widely distributed, clean, and climate-benign," adding, "No other energy source has all of these attributes."[3]

The Advantages of Wind Power

Wind is indeed an inexhaustible energy source. Winds are created by the sun, which heats up regions of Earth unevenly. This uneven heating creates air pressure imbalances. As highly pressurized air rushes toward low-pressure regions, wind is created. This source of power has been used since ancient times. Thousands of years before the birth of Jesus, ancient Egyptians rigged sails to their reed boats to navigate the Nile under favorable winds. With the invention of the windmill in the Middle Ages, the power of the wind was put to work to grind grain and pump water. In modern times wind energy has been employed mainly to drive electric turbines. As the wind strikes the turbine's blades, they rotate, driving a rotor, which then powers a generator. The electricity produced by the generator can be

This wind turbine sits atop a barren hill in California. A clean energy source, wind power can always be replenished.

used to power homes directly or sent to the utility grid for use by other electricity consumers.

Many energy companies are currently investing in wind technologies. According to the American Wind Energy Association (AWEA), in 2005 some twenty-five hundred megawatts of wind-

A technician walks under the rotor of a wind generator. Many experts expect wind power to become a major energy source of the future.

The Parts and Pieces of a Wind Turbine

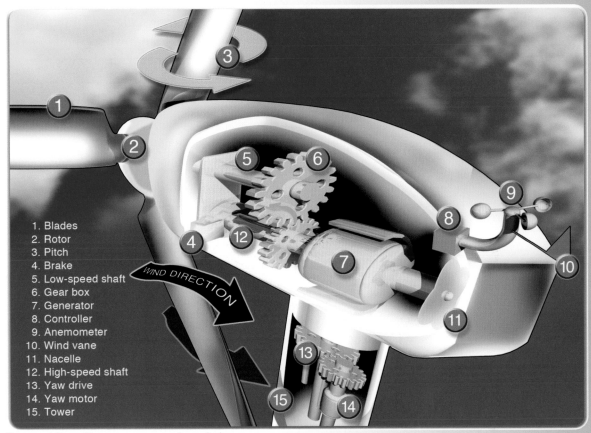

1. Blades
2. Rotor
3. Pitch
4. Brake
5. Low-speed shaft
6. Gear box
7. Generator
8. Controller
9. Anemometer
10. Wind vane
11. Nacelle
12. High-speed shaft
13. Yaw drive
14. Yaw motor
15. Tower

WIND DIRECTION

Source: Alliant Energy. www.powerhousekids.com.

generated electric power were installed, enough to supply the needs of half a million homes. Wind turbines have been a boon to rural communities, many experts believe. Turbines can be erected on windy agricultural lands, producing electricity—and hence, money—for farmers. According to the Sierra Club, one of the nation's oldest environmental organizations,

As a growing power source, wind energy can become a major force for economic development. Wind development can save consumers money and bring construction jobs, leasing royalties, and increased tax revenues to local communities. Supplying even 5 percent of the country's electricity with wind power by 2020 would add $60 billion in capital investment in rural America, provide $1.2 billion in new income for farmers and rural landowners, and create 80,000 new jobs. Farmers and ranchers can also use wind power as a new "crop," earning $2,000 per year in lease payments per turbine, helping insulate them from falling commodity prices. [4]

Farms are not the only windy places being eyed by wind energy companies. Plans are also under way to erect wind turbines along the nation's coastlines to take advantage of steady sea breezes. By some estimates, offshore wind generators could eventually supply enough electricity to meet all U.S. energy needs. Oil fields, too, have become prime locations for wind farms. Wind turbines are being installed in oil fields in Texas, where they generate electricity as the oil wells pump oil. Indeed, as AWEA executive director Randall Swisher concludes, "The wind power industry is stepping up to provide the U.S. with a significant amount of its power needs in this time of uncertainty." [5]

The Disadvantages of Wind Power

Despite these advantages, wind energy has many critics. One of the criticisms leveled at wind power is its unreliability. The wind does not blow constantly in all places at all times, opponents point out. Often, it is too weak to turn turbine blades, even in windy regions. At other times the wind is too strong; if the turbines are not turned off, strong winds can damage or destroy them. The erratic nature of wind power means that communities must purchase expensive backup generators or storage batteries to ensure an uninterrupted supply of electricity.

Other commentators object to wind power being called an environmentally friendly energy source. They argue that the blades of windmills present a danger to birds. Most critics point to the wind farm at Altamont Pass in California as a prime example of this problem. With some five thousand wind turbines operating in the hills of northern California, Altamont

Pass generates enough electricity to power 200,000 homes. Since its inception in the 1980s, however, Altamont Pass has gained a reputation as the deadliest wind farm in the nation. The whirling blades kill thousands of birds, including many eagles and other raptors, each year. According to the Center for Biological Diversity, "Wind turbines at the Altamont Pass

Critics say that turbine blades, like those used at a wind farm in Tehachapi Pass, California, pose dangers to birds.

Opponents of wind turbines speak out at a public hearing. Some people think windmills ruin the beauty of nature.

Wind Resource Area (APWRA) kill more birds of prey than any other wind facility in North America, due to their location on a major bird migratory route in an area with high concentrations of raptors, including the highest density of breeding golden eagles in the world."[6]

Many critics also oppose wind energy on the grounds that erecting turbines tall enough to capture the wind mars the beauty of landscapes. In Great Britain, where the government has set a national goal that 20 percent of its energy will come from renewables by 2020, a battle rages over the increasing number of turbines that have been built there. People opposed to the wind farms argue that the turbines blight the countryside. In the United States, too, controversy has erupted over the siting of turbines. Opponents are protesting a proposal to build a wind farm in Nantucket Sound off Cape Cod in Massachusetts. A group called the Alliance to Protect Nantucket Sound has campaigned vigorously to block the offshore wind project. The group argues that building the farm would destroy the natural beauty of the area. According to the group, "Nantucket Sound and the waters surrounding the Cape and Islands are famous for natural beauty and abundant, diverse and unique wildlife. . . . Nantucket Sound is central to our entire economy precisely because of its natural appeal. . . . It is a natural treasure and it must be preserved."[7] The group has gone to court to fight the wind farm and has even lobbied Congress to halt the project on national security grounds. It argues that the wind turbines may interfere with military radar and allow small planes to cross undetected into U.S. airspace. Because of this opposition, the building of the Nantucket wind farm remains uncertain.

Windmills Make a Comeback

Notwithstanding these criticisms of wind power, it remains a popular energy source. Perhaps no better evidence of its popularity can be found than the Bush administration's inclusion of wind power in its energy plan. Bush's stance on the issue signals a consensus among Americans of all political affiliations that the nation cannot continue to depend on fossil fuels indefinitely. The era of fossil fuels, which put an end to reliance on windmills to pump water and grind grain, could be coming to an end itself. Once again, the globe may be dotted with windmills, helping the world's people do their work.

Notes

1. George W. Bush, "The 2006 State of the Union Speech," January 31, 2006. www.whitehouse.gov.

2. U.S. Department of Energy, "Advantages and Disadvantages of Wind Energy," August 30, 2005. http://eereweb.ee.doe.gov/windandhydro/wind_ad.html.

3. Lester R. Brown, "Wind Power Set to Become World's Leading Energy Source," Earth Policy Institute, June 25, 2003. www.earth-policy.org/Updates/Update24.htm.

4. Sierra Club, "Clean Power Comes On Strong," undated. www.sierraclub.org/globalwarming/cleanenergy/renewables factsheet.pdf.

5. Quoted in Christine Real de Azua, "U.S. Wind Industry to Break Installation Records, Expand by More Than 35% in 2005," November 3, 2005. www.awea.org/news/US_wind_industry_to_break_installation_records_110305.html.

6. Center for Biological Diversity, "Clean Wind Energy at Altamont Pass?" www.biologicaldiversity.org/swcbd/programs/bdes/altamont/altamont.html.

7. Alliance to Protect Nantucket Sound, "The Sound: Overview," undated. www.saveoursound.com/Sound.

This German windmill is a typical example of early European windmills, which were key to the development of civilization in Europe.

CHAPTER 1

The Development of Wind Power

Ancient Sails Harness the Wind

Leo Block

People first captured wind energy with the sail. In the following selection, marine historian Leo Block recounts the origins of the sail and how it was first used to power ships. He credits the ancient Egyptians with inventing the first sailing vessel, perhaps as early as 6000 B.C. The Egyptian boats, made of bundled reeds, were difficult to maneuver, but several centuries later, Egypt's shipwrights learned how to make stronger, more maneuverable boats out of wood. Before long, Egyptian sailors ventured into the Mediterranean Sea, where they discovered routes to Syria and Crete. Sailing vessels would prove to be the most important wind-powered technology in history, leading to global exploration, trade, and conquest. Leo Block is a retired U.S. Navy captain, mechanical engineer, and historian. He sails his 30-foot (9m) sloop off the coast of Southern California.

T he exact origin of the sail is still disputed by historians. Some contend that the sail was originated on the River Nile or evolved independently in Egypt and Indonesia. Others believe that the sail existed earlier in the maritime island cultures, in Bahrain in the Arabian Gulf and in Malta in the Mediterranean.

The earliest documentary evidence of a sailing craft is a crude painting on an Egyptian vase that dates back to 6000 B.C. A better description is provided by an Egyptian wall painting circa 4700 B.C. that shows a hull made of papyrus reed bundles (the boat in which the infant Moses was hidden on the bank of the Nile was also made of papyrus reeds). The bundles were lashed together to form an overhanging bow and stern. A fore-and-aft truss was required to raise the bow and stern. A single tall rectangular sail is mounted on an A-type mast as shown in figure 1 [below]; a conventional pole mast would have penetrated through the bottom of a reed hull.

The forward location of the mast permitted sailing only in downwind direction (sailing ahead of the wind and probably a little to each side). An attempt to sail in any other direction would force the bow in a downwind direction. With the wind from any direction except astern, it was necessary to lower the sail and rely on paddles for propulsion. Sailing only downwind was satisfactory to the early Egyptians as the prevailing wind blew upstream on the Nile. They would sail upstream and for the return journey, take the sail down and paddle downstream with the current.

Shipbuilders Switch to Wood

By 3000 B.C. the reed hull was replaced with a wood hull made of cedar imported from present-day Lebanon. The wood hull allowed the use of oars as the wood permitted the installation

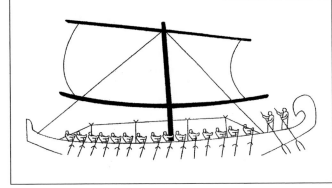

Figure 1. Egyptian reed hull sailing vessel, 4700 B.C., for sailing upstream and paddling downstream on the Nile (left).

Figure 2. Egyptian wood hull sailing vessel, 1600 B.C. In vessels of this type the Egyptians sailed the Mediterranean and along the east coast of Africa.

of a fulcrum (the pivot point support) required by an oar. A fulcrum was not feasible on a hull constructed of reeds. . . .

By 1600 B.C. the Egyptians centered the mast and made the sail lower and wider, but the mast was still without shrouds (side supports). A lower yard was added to permit sheeting the sail to the still narrow hull [figure 2 on p. 21]. Lowering the sail reduced the heeling (leaning to the downwind side) effect and probably permitted sailing with a quartering wind (45 degrees from astern). A wind 50 degrees from the stern would be prohibitive because the spoon-shaped hull provided very little lateral resist-

Ancient Egyptian sailors traversed the waters of the Nile in wooden barges similar to this model. Wind has been harnessed for energy for thousands of years.

ance and the vessel would slide on the surface of the water in a downwind (leeward) direction.

These vessels were seventy feet long, seventeen to eighteen feet wide; fully laden they had a draft of about three feet. They required fifteen oarsmen on each side and two or three steering oars on each side. The lower yard was supported by eight individual lines on each side of the mast as the sail cloth was not strong enough to support the weight of the lower yard. The halyards (ropes) that supported the lower yard were looped over a frame attached to the top of the mast and had to be hoisted against the friction of the frame, as the sheave or pulley was not yet invented.

Sailing the Ocean with Primitive Vessels

In these primitive vessels the Egyptians, in addition to sailing the Nile River, made remarkable ocean passages. The voyage to Syria, made as early as 2480 B.C., required paddling, and later rowing, as it was directly into the eye of the wind. Navigation consisted of following the coast on their right-hand side. The return trip was downwind and made under sail. Eventually the Egyptians voyaged to Crete, a distance of about four hundred miles, which required them to be out of sight of land for five or six days. . . .

This basic sail of the Egyptians was ultimately adopted by the Phoenicians, Greeks, and Romans. It is believed that even the nations of the East learned shipbuilding from the Egyptians, who are justifiably credited with the establishment of the art of naval architecture.

How Windmills Helped the Dutch Reclaim the Netherlands

Suzanne Beedell

In the selection that follows, Suzanne Beedell describes the key role that windmills have played in Dutch history. Much of the Netherlands lies below sea level. In the Middle Ages the Dutch used windmills to scoop water out of low-lying areas, up canals, and then into rivers or the ocean. Beedell describes how the Dutch adapted grain-grinding windmills to pump water. Early versions, developed in the fifteenth century, had large wooden scoop wheels at their base. Linked in a series, the windmills drained lakes and marshes, allowing the Dutch to farm the reclaimed land. The Dutch also used windmills for a variety of other purposes, including crushing seeds for oil and sawing timber. Today, Holland's windmills serve as a tourist attraction and as a defense against the possibility that modern electrical pumps will fail in a blackout. Suzanne Beedell is the author of numerous books on a wide variety of subjects.

No other country has so many windmills as Holland. Everywhere across the flat lands, under the wide bright skies there are hundreds of huge, solid, strong windmills, like the Dutch themselves, dominating the landscape in which they live. Even in stillness they are impressive, but turning in a stiff breeze from the cold North Sea these big mills give an impression of power unequalled by any other man-made machine.

Of old, the Dutch lived in a country constantly menaced by water—by the sea and by the rivers of Europe flooding the low-lying land. They used the wind, the other great element which swept round them, to fight the water. By converting their grinding mills (first recorded early in the thirteenth century) to pumping mills (first recorded in 1414), they began the work—which is still going on, although no longer by windpower—of reclaiming huge areas of land from the sea. The windmill continued to be used for drainage of reclaimed land up to the present century, when oil and steam engines gradually replaced the mills.

The Dutch realised that, as each mill became derelict, a vital part of their heritage was disappearing and completely altering the look of their countryside. One irreplaceable complex of fifty was dismantled in the 1930s to make way for modern pumps. The new polders, made with modern machinery not windmills, have a strangely bare look compared with the old windmill areas of Holland. Of the 9,000 windmills which existed in the nineteenth century, about 1,000 remain today, and the work of restoration and preservation continues.

How Windmills Drained the Land

To drain a large area, the Dutch first dug a dyke and a ring canal round it, and then at intervals installed windmills to lift water from the lake into the ring canal. The height of the lift is governed by the radius of the scoop wheel, usually about 5 ft (diameter 10 ft). The mills would work away until they had lowered the level of the lake by 5 ft. Then another series of mills were installed at that level to lift water from 5 ft lower down to a series of catchment areas; from there the original mills would pump it into the ring canals. This was repeated until the deepest pools were drained. The water in the ring canal, at a comparatively high level, could then be drained away by gravity, or if necessary by further pumping, into the river systems, and eventually into the sea. In this way *molengang* sets of windmills were built up to drain the polders into the canals and rivers. At Kinderdijk, near Alblasserdam, there are sixteen polder mills all

Windmills dot the landscape along a canal in the Netherlands, known for its many types of windmills and many ways of using them.

together. They do not work all the time, although once a year they are all set going—a truly wonderful sight. One mill is always kept working for the benefit of tourists.

The earliest pumping mills were hollow post mills. They were developed from the ordinary type of trestle post mill used for grinding throughout northern Europe, which varied little in principle and only in regional detail. However, to transfer the drive of a post mill to a scoop wheel was obviously difficult because the whole body of the mill turned on its post while the scoop wheel must remain fixed in its basin. To overcome this problem, the Dutch balanced the mill on a hollow post and carried the drive down through this by means of a separate shaft. The wip mill [a type of Dutch pumping mill] has a buck on a tall post, proportionally smaller than that of a trestle post mill, and round the post is a thatched house enclosing the crown wheel at the bottom of the vertical shaft and the verti-cal pit wheel geared to it. The rest of the roundhouse is taken up by the miller's living quarters. It always has two doors so that one can get in and out whichever way the buck and sweeps are turned. But there is not much room in there, so if the miller has a big family he needs a cottage as well!

The Development of Polder Mills

Next evolved the very much bigger polder mill. This is an octagonal smock mill with thatched sides (thatching reed was, of course, available everywhere in the marshes) and a moveable cap. A polder mill has a brick or wooden base and inside this the scoop wheel. The thatching on a wooden frame meant that the mill was much lighter than if it were made entirely of brick; on the soft Dutch subsoil this was an important factor. The concave sides of the polder mill look very beautiful, but there is a practical reason for their incurving shape: the wind, pushed ahead and sideways by the descending sail, meets less resistance than from a straight-sided mill.

How Polder Mills Drain Low-Lying Areas

The diagram shows how a succession of windmills is used to transfer water from a low-lying area, or polder, into a canal. Mill 1 pumps the water to the level of Mill 2, which pumps the water to Mill 3. Mill 3 then pumps the water over a dyke and into a canal, where it is diverted to a river or the sea.

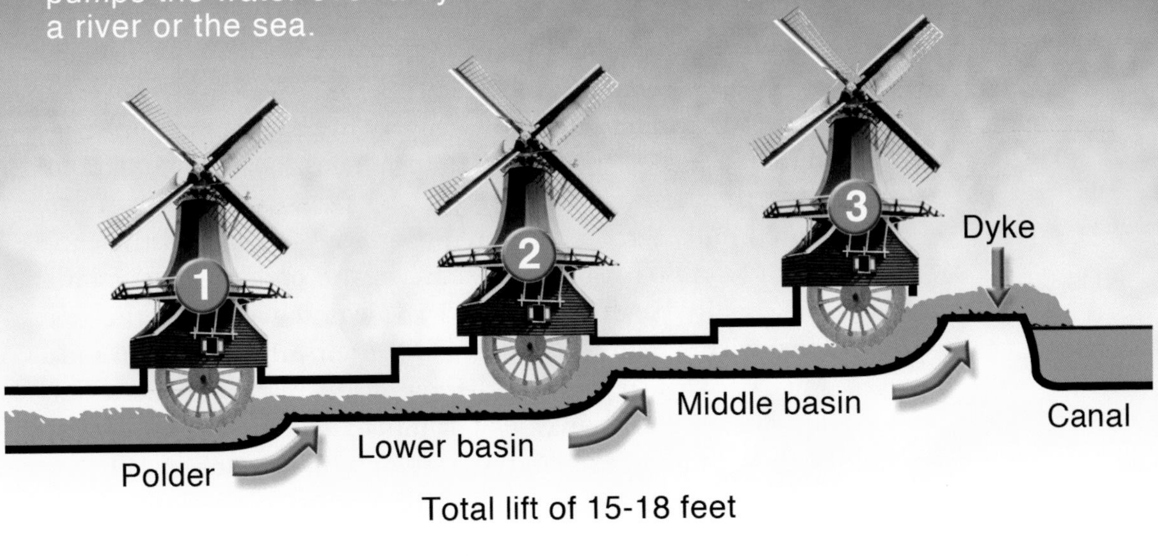

Dyke

Middle basin

Canal

Lower basin

Polder

Total lift of 15-18 feet

Villagers skate near a windmill in this winter scene from a Dutch painting. Windmills were crucial to life in the Netherlands.

Because a polder mill contains very little machinery in relation to its size, half the ground floor can be used as a living room and the first floor is the bedroom.

Dutch mills carry a decorated board on the front of the cap, called a *beard*. This bears the date of the building of the mill and is usually beautifully carved and painted. Despite the gay colours with which the Dutch paint their mills, common sails of dark canvas are usual and show up in black silhouette for miles when set; this gives Dutch mills a much more menacing look than those in England with their white shuttered sails.

Apart from the wip mill and the polder mill, which are specifically drainage mills, several other types are common. To grind corn, the ordinary post mill of the Low Countries—with either an open trestle or a roundhouse, and a tall buck—was used from the earliest days. In Holland it frequently had a thatched cap.

Brick tower grinding mills, again with thatched caps, also survive. Most impressive of all are the colossal tower mills, each encircled by a working stage half-way or even higher up the tower. Because Holland is so flat, small man-made mounds were raised to carry windmills; even then—especially in towns where other tall buildings took too much wind away from the mill—the Dutch had to build high. In these huge mills, the bottom of the tower made a splendid house for the miller; above the circular stage, the brick tower would be continued to cap level, or a smock mill—outwardly like the polder mill—with concave thatched sides, would be built on top of the brick tower.

Various Types of Mills Have Different Uses

There were also various types of grinding mills for chalk, dye, cocoa, tan, spices and cement; and mills which pressed oil from mustard and other seeds, leaving a residue of hard cake to be used for animal feed.

An *edge mill* was used to grind chalk, etc, and also seeds for oil production before they were put through the stamping machinery. The mill consisted of two runner stones set on edge on a horizontal spindle which passed through the main vertical spindle from the stone nut. These two stones, one set nearer to the central spindle than the other, rotated and rolled upon a solid pan. The material on the pan was guided into the stone by wooden guides and, when it was sufficiently pulverised, the gate could be opened through which it could be brushed into a receptacle below.

In the *oil mill* a vertical cam wheel on a heavy horizontal shaft was driven by the crown wheel at the bottom of the main vertical shaft coming down from the wallower. This cam shaft rotated the cams thus causing a series of rams and stamps to rise and fall upon

This windmill at Kinderdijk is a prime example of the well-preserved windmills of the Netherlands.

the meal (from the seeds previously ground in the edge mill), which had been heated and put into a special bag. It would first be pressed by means of wedges beaten by the rams, then taken out, broken up into pieces and put into pots beneath the stamps.

Sawmills were also common in Holland, and can still be found. The smaller ones used the wind to turn circular saws, but the larger mills could cope with the heaviest sawing jobs. . . .

Big smock mills are used to cut big trees. The light *paltrok* mills, which have wooden wings at their sides to accommodate long balks of timber, cut small trees or previously split timber. The paltrok mill is built of wood round a king post, with the whole body supported on a curb on the top of a circular brick

Dutch windmills are practical as well as beautiful. In the event of massive power failure, the windmills can still be used to pump water.

wall. In principle, this is not unlike the British turret mill, except that the supporting wall is low and the body of the mill is correspondingly tall. It is winded by means of a capstan attached to a low stage at the back of the mill.

Preserving Dutch Windmills

The Dutch have made strenuous efforts to prevent any more of their mills becoming derelict, and to restore and repair mills wherever possible. Millers who keep their mills working are subsidised by help with upkeep. Fortunately Dutch mills are so big that they can be modernised and turned into dwellings without the exterior being altered or spoiled. Other mills have become local museums, or reception centres for visitors; in Holland, some useful purpose is always found which will allow the mill to be saved. In a country where great areas would soon be flooded if pumping ceased, a failure of electric supply for any reason over any length of time could be utterly disastrous, if sufficient windmills were not available to take over. Some are therefore kept in working order at strategic points, under the provisions of the Act for the Protection of Waterways in Wartime. During World War II the windmills took over a lot of pumping work, and a great deal of grinding also went on where electric power was not available.

How Windmills Helped Pioneers Settle the American Southwest

T. Lindsay Baker

In the following selection historian T. Lindsay Baker describes how windmills made it possible for pioneers to settle the vast, semiarid expanses of Texas. Settlers arriving in Texas recognized the need for a way to pump water, but the first use of windmills in the Lone Star State, according to Baker, was to grind grain. For this purpose, European-style windmills were erected in various locations around the state. However, such windmills were too bulky and expensive to be useful to pump water. The need for a lightweight, efficient windmill was eventually met by the invention of a Connecticut mechanic. His windmill, patented in the 1850s, became immensely popular. These windmills, which could survive storms and needed little maintenance, proved essential to the settlement of the western portion of the state, where surface water was (and still is) scarce. T. Lindsay Baker began his working life as an attendant on a passenger railroad and went on to earn a doctorate in history from Texas Tech University. He is director of the Texas Heritage Museum in Hillsboro.

T. Lindsay Baker, "Windmills in Texas," *The Hidden History of Texas*, www.texan cultures.utsa.edu, January 28, 2006. Copyright © 2001 The University of Texas Institute of Texas Cultures at San Antonio. Reproduced by permission.

"The great want of Texas is sufficient water," wrote a resident of the Lone Star State in 1860, adding, "There is a million dollars lying waiting for the first man who will bring us . . . a windmill, strong, durable and controllable." Little did that writer know that such machines not only existed but that they also were already in Texas.

The story of the use of wind goes back to the beginnings of recorded history. From time immemorial, humans have used the wind blowing on sails to propel boats and ships across the water. Most historians of wind power agree that people first applied the wind long ago to grind grain in the Middle East. Some historians tell us that Europeans first saw windmills doing this type of work in the Middle East during the 1100s, and that they took the idea of building such wind machines back to Europe. Other scholars think that windmills developed

independently in Europe. Whichever the case, Europeans perfected wind power technology to create the picturesque four-bladed windmills familiar today in Holland, England, France, and Germany.

Windmills Come to Texas

European immigrants brought the idea of these Old World windmills to Texas; a number of them appeared across the state during the middle 1800s. German immigrant Max Kreuger remembered working at a windmill in Helena in

Riders on horseback travel across a Texas ranch. Early pioneers of the Lone Star State erected windmills to pump water.

Karnes County [in south central Texas] in the winter of 1868–69:

> I had intended to earn my living as a cowboy, but as herding and corralling the cattle did not begin until springtime I was forced to consider other means of livelihood at least for the time being. I began grinding corn, using a primitive Dutch windmill for power. . . .

European-style windmills like the ones at Helena and Victoria, Texas, were expensive to build. They required a lot of labor to erect, and grindstones were costly to purchase. After the mills were erected, they required constant attention to operate. If they ran too fast, they would tear apart or catch on fire from the heat created by friction on their wooden bearings. When the wind changed direction, the miller had to rotate the mill so that the blades again would face the wind. Even the act of stretching fabric over the wooden-slat blades took a lot of time and effort, not to mention agility. Nothing about operating the traditional European-style windmills was either efficient or cheap. This situation led to the development of a new type of windmill in America.

Customizing European Windmills for Use in the American Southwest

In the early 1850s, a pump repairman in Connecticut suggested to a local mechanic named Daniel Halladay that some of his customers could really use a wind machine that needed no special human attention to pump water from the ground. Halladay realized that his friend had a good idea, and he set his mind to the task. In 1854 he successfully invented a windmill that could pump water without human attention. It turned to face the changing wind directions and automatically regulated its own speed of operation. This meant that his windmill was self-regulating. Halladay got a government patent to protect his rights to the new invention, and, within a short time, with others organized a company to produce his Halladay Standard Windmills.

European immigrants brought their mill technology to Texas. This historic windmill is in Victoria.

Halladay's company began manufacturing and selling windmills. As soon as potential customers learned that self-regulating windmills could pump their water and do other valuable work without requiring constant attention, they started buying the machines. Railway companies almost immediately saw use for windmills in pumping fresh water from the ground for their steam locomotives, and they also wanted them.

One of the first self-governing windmills used in Texas was Mitchell's Patent windmill, invented and patented by James Mitchell of Woodsfield, Ohio, in 1857. Mr. E.D. Nash of Columbia, Texas, by 1860 was the sales agent in Texas for

Mitchell's windmill. He advertised it in newspapers across the state, as well as in the *Texas Almanac*, advising potential customers that they could view the mills in operation pumping water for locomotives at stations on both the Houston and Texas Central Railroad and the Houston Tap and Brazoria Railroad. Nash claimed of his self-regulating wind machine, "once set up and put to running, it needs no attention, but will operate the year round like a thing of life."

A variation on the old European windmill, this wheel-style windmill and silo operate in San Antonio, Texas.

Self-Regulating Windmills

Both Halladay's and Mitchell's windmills had wind wheels comprising large paddle-shaped blades which automatically varied their pitch [angle] to control the speed of operation. In time this design changed to one with wind wheels comprising multiple sections of thin wooden blades which pivoted [turned] out of the wind to regulate wheel speed. This governing of speed protected the machines from self-destruction from centrifugal [fast-spinning] force during high winds. Because the wheels consisted of sections of blades, they were called sectional-wheel windmills.

The other large category of windmills used in Texas were called solid-wheel windmills, which had a different design. The wheels were rigid, or "solid," and did not have pivoting [turning] sections. In governing, the entire wheels of the solid wheel windmills inclined away from increasing winds. They did this because they were slightly off center or because they had small side vanes parallel with the wheels which pushed them out of the wind. Solid wheel windmills generally had hinged vanes, or tails, which remained parallel with the wind direction all the time. As the wheels pivoted away from increasing winds, linkage raised weighted levers or placed pressure on springs which brought the wheels back to face the wind squarely when its velocity [speed] decreased. To this day sectional wheel and solid wheel windmills constitute the majority of all wind machines manufactured and used.

Mass Production

The Civil War and the times of unrest and economic dislocation following the conflict delayed the further introduction of windmills to Texas. By the 1870s, however, mass-produced factory-made wind machines from the midwestern states began coming to Texas in increasing numbers. The heyday [high point] for their use in Texas, however, came between the 1880s and the 1910s. During this time the spinning wheels came to dot the Texas landscape from East Texas all the way west of the Pecos.

Access to Underground Water

Windmills had a very real impact on the settlement of the western two-thirds of Texas. Without mechanically drilled wells and windmills to pump water from them, people were forced to live in areas that had running water from streams or springs. As they moved westward across Texas, they were forced to occupy only the limited number of areas with "live" water on the surface of the land. By drilling wells and securing water pumped with windmills, however, people could live almost anywhere in semi-arid western Texas, where water usually was available underground. Consequently, windmills made possible a much more even distribution of population across drier West Texas than would have taken place if people had been forced to live only where they found streams or springs.

Although no statistics on the number of windmills used in Texas are available, the letters written by Texans who used them shed some important light on their role in the economic development of the state. W.P. Gillespie at Trinity University in Tehuacana, Texas, on February 18, 1875, wrote that he was very pleased with his Halladay Standard windmill and declared the invention to be "a national blessing." He added that "it will be the prime agent in rendering the wide and desolate prairies of our western border habitable and aid man in reclaiming and bringing into cultivation the arid sands."

From San Angelo S.E. Couch reported in 1890 that he was using his 18-foot-diameter Perkins solid-wheel windmill over a 350-foot-deep well, which, in his words, "has now been running over two years, watering no less than 6,000 head of sheep, stock, horses, etc., and is my only dependence for water, having no running water or permanent water holes."

About 1881 Charles H. Nimitz, proprietor of the Nimitz Hotel in Fredericksburg, Texas, wrote that he was using a 12-foot Challenge sectional-wheel windmill to pump water from a 72-foot-deep well and then force it horizontally 450 feet. He reported that his windmill "runs with very light wind, and no storm, not even our much feared 'Texas Northers,' seems to hurt it."

Windmills Help to Water the Cattle

The best-known use of windmills in Texas through the years has been in pumping water for livestock. In West Texas windmills made living in most upland areas possible. Then, as the marketing of livestock changed from a per-head basis to a per-pound basis, stock raisers began drilling additional wells and

Early settlers in the dry climate of West Texas relied on windmills to pump underground water.

A common sight throughout West Texas, longhorn cattle graze near broken windmills. Ranchers used windmills to pump water for cattle.

installing more windmills so cattle did not have to walk more than about two miles to water. Otherwise the animals "walked off" their weight getting to the water. To meet this need, ranchers installed thousands upon thousands of windmills to pump water to the surface from drilled wells.

Still Operating

Windmills have remained an integral part of life in rural Texas to the present time. In virtually every county, windmillers still install and repair water-pumping windmills. Often they combine this work with that of general well service and pump repair. Many telephone directories in Texas towns still list entries under the category "windmills."

Windmills have played a major role in the economic development of Texas since the 1860s, and to this day they remain important elements of rural living for many Texans. The attachment of Texans to windmills is more than just economic and utilitarian. Texans feel a great fondness and even love for them. Journalists Claude and Carolyn Crowley of Fort Worth expressed the feelings of many Texans for their windmills this way:

> . . . it's clear that the windmill's appeal spans the generations. The beauty of its spare frame and spinning wheel satisfies the eye, and its clanks, squeaks and gurgles please the ear. Each windmill forms a cherished link—a sort of historical monument—with our pioneer past.

CHAPTER 2

Does Wind Power Benefit the Environment?

Wind Turbines Kill Too Many Birds

Andrew Chapman

In the selection that follows, Australian engineer Andrew Chapman condemns the slaughter of thousands of birds of prey by wind turbines. Wind farms, where large numbers of electricity-generating windmills are clustered, have had a disastrous effect on avian wildlife, he says. The wind farm at Altamont Pass, California, kills hundreds of eagles, hawks, and owls each year, Chapman claims. Moreover, the mere presence of the huge, whirling blades disturbs birds living up to 0.5 miles (0.8km) away. A newer wind farm at Starfish Hill, in South Australia, is even more lethal than is Altamont Pass, Chapman argues. Considering the toll that such facilities take on wildlife, to call wind energy environmentally friendly is wrong, he asserts. A better course, he argues, would be to make direct use of solar power, which has none of the life-threatening side effects of wind power. Andrew Chapman is a consulting engineer who has served on the Conservation Advisory Committee of Australia's regional government in the state of Victoria.

Bird kills at wind farms are in fact significant and this is particularly relevant because wind power companies market themselves as providing "green energy." This image, of their own creation and naively fostered by others, should not exempt them from the normal level of environmental scrutiny and compliance applied to industry. Company boards, investors and consumers alike want to be sure that their expectations of social

Andrew Chapman, "Renewable Energy Industry Environmental Impacts," www.countryguardian.net, November 15, 2003. Reproduced by permission of the author.

and environmental responsibility are met and not just by ticking boxes on paper. It is therefore important that the impact of wind farms on the environment, particularly wildlife, be conveyed so people have the opportunity to make informed social and environmentally conscious investment decisions.

The impact of wind farms on wildlife is worth [mentioning] as the wind industry well knows there have been some disastrous consequences for wildlife. The United States Fish and Wildlife Service estimates that the Altamont Pass wind farm in California, constructed around

Located in a raptor migration corridor, the wind farm in Altamont Pass, California (below), can be harmful to avian wildlife like this Golden Eagle (left).

1970, kills 300 eagles, hawks, kites and other raptors each year, and of these, 60 are Golden Eagles. It wasn't until the late 1980s and early 1990s that the magnitude of bird kills at wind farms was discovered and this was because monitoring of impact on birds had generally been poor and removal of carcasses by scavengers meant few observations were made of kills. It is standard practice to determine impact by looking at bird kill rates per turbine. The US Fish and Wildlife Service gives bird kill rate estimates in Europe of up to 37 birds/turbine/year and bird kill estimates in USA at an average of 2.19 birds/turbine/year with raptor kill rates at an average of 0.033 raptors/turbine/year. The US Fish and Wildlife Service suggest these figures may be a considerable underestimate.

The Australian Wind Energy Association's response to the Altamont raptor kills is, "In those days obligations on development were far looser than they are today, particularly in Australia where the potential impact of any wind farm development is scrutinised by regulatory authorities including Environment Australia at the Commonwealth level. Besides this, such a concentration of eagles found at Altamont does not occur anywhere in Australia and neither is the geography comparable."

Research by [avian expert] J. [E.] Winkleman has shown that resident birds could be affected for distances of between 250–500 metres from turbines with disturbance causing between a 60% and 95% decline in bird usage close to the turbines and that 1.0 megawatt turbines affect larger water birds such as ducks and swans for up to 800 metres. In Europe the consequence of bird avoidance behaviour is considered even more significant than the bird kills.

The Australian Wind Energy Association says the "The U.K. Royal Society for the Protection of Birds [RSPB] supports wind energy" but on 15 August 2003 Peter Exley of the RSPB had this to say about wind farms:

The RSPB recognises that inappropriately sited wind farms can cause problems for birds. It is precisely because of this that since 1998 the society has objected to 26 wind farm proposals (on and offshore). . . .

Scherer. ©2005 by Randy Scherer. Reproduced by permission

The RSPB strongly supports the sustainable development of wind power and other forms of renewable energy as a means of helping to tackle climate change, which we regard as the biggest long-term threat to the environment. The available evidence, from the UK and elsewhere, suggests that wind farms that are appropriately sited do not pose a significant hazard for birds. The RSPB will, and does, object to development proposals, including wind farms, that threaten important birds and their habitats. . . .

High Fatality Rate

When it was discovered that wind farms in the USA were killing Golden Eagles (*Aquila chrysaetos*) it was thought that in Australia Wedge-tailed Eagles (*Aquila Audax*) would also be susceptible since the two species are closely related. I recently received the following information from members of the

Eaglehawk Conservation Group in South Australia about the Starfish Hill wind farm, a facility developed by Starfish Hill Wind Farm Pty Ltd, a wholly owned subsidiary of Tarong Energy, based in Queensland:

> On 22 September 2003 the group said a Wedge-tailed Eagle had been killed at the Starfish Hill wind farm. This kill occurred before it was officially opened by Premier Mike Rann on Saturday 4 October 03.
>
> During the first week in October 2003 a second eagle was found dead under one of the turbines by the Tarong Energy Site Manager.

At least four months after the first turbine commenced operating and even after the last kill there was no official bird kill monitoring procedure in place. These two eagle kills are known only because members of the public have stumbled across them.

There is now enough information to compare the environmental performance of the wind farms of Starfish Hill and Altamont. Starfish Hill has 23 turbines and the turbines have killed 2 eagles within a 4 month period, which extrapolates to 6 per year giving a kill rate of 0.26 raptors/turbine/year. At Altamont, where there are 6,700 turbines, 300 raptors are killed per year; the kill rate is 0.045 raptors/turbine/year. The figures show the Starfish Hill turbines to be nearly six times more lethal on raptors than Altamont. If the impacts on the genus *Aquila* are compared, then Starfish Hill is nearly 30 times worse than Altamont. This exercise reveals that the environmental performance of the Starfish Hill wind farm is worse than the worst wind farm in the world for killing raptors. For other bird groups are we also to experience the high kill rates (37 birds/turbine/year) found in Europe?

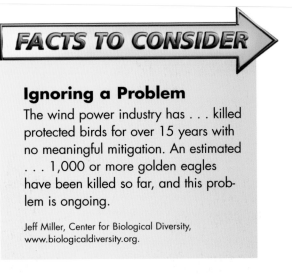

FACTS TO CONSIDER

Ignoring a Problem

The wind power industry has . . . killed protected birds for over 15 years with no meaningful mitigation. An estimated . . . 1,000 or more golden eagles have been killed so far, and this problem is ongoing.

Jeff Miller, Center for Biological Diversity, www.biologicaldiversity.org.

Evaluations of the bird kills at Altamont suggested that the small, 18 metre diameter rotor, turbines rotating at high speed, 60 revolutions per minute, were a major contributor. It has previously been suggested that the larger (70 metre diameter rotor) rotating at the lower speed (30 revolutions per minute) being used in Australia would cause less problems for birds. Whilst the rotational speed of the larger turbines is less, the blade speed is a more important criteria for birds, particularly raptors, because they cannot readily detect movement across their path as they approach the object. A simple calculation reveals that the larger turbines, although rotating at

Solar panels (pictured) harness the sun's energy without risk to wildlife.

half the speed of the smaller models, have double the tip speed. That is, there is much more swept area that birds cannot readily detect, possibly accounting for the high fatality rate for raptors at Starfish Hill. . . .

Wind farms depend on subsidy and when the subsidy goes so will the turbines, except for the large immoveable heavily reinforced concrete foundation blocks left scattered across farms to remind everyone of this foolish folly. In the meantime any wind farms constructed would contribute to an ongoing destruction of our native birds. . . .

Solar Energy Preferable

Wind energy is second hand solar energy—that is, the wind is derived from the sun heating the earth's surface at different rates and times to cause surface air movements. During this process a considerable amount of the energy from solar radiation is lost to other energy sinks, so it makes sense to capture solar radiation in the first instance. Using solar radiation to heat hot water systems and generate electricity, as has been done on house roofs throughout Australia for many years, results in minimal environmental impact that can at least be monitored by the consumer. Australia is a world leader in developing solar energy technology whereas wind power technology and equipment is imported. . . .

Clearly there are negative environmental impacts from wind farms and they do not deserve the label "green". The use of this misleading promotional jargon should be stopped.

2 Wind Turbines Kill Relatively Few Birds

Mick Sagrillo

In the following selection a wind energy expert challenges the claim that wind turbines cause the deaths of too many birds. Mick Sagrillo argues that structures other than wind turbines are responsible for the vast majority of fatal in-flight collisions. Additionally, loss of natural habitat and pesticides account for more deaths than do wind farms. The deaths of a number of golden eagles and other raptors at Altamont Pass in northern California have attracted a lot of negative attention, Sagrillo notes, but he says that the situation there is not typical of commercial wind farms. Most farms, he notes, are not built in a raptor migration corridor. Mick Sagrillo is an expert columnist for the American Wind Energy Association's newsletter and the owner of Sagrillo Power and Light, a consulting firm specializing in home-sized wind turbine technology.

Electricity generated from renewable energy resources is an environmentally-preferred alternative to conventionally produced electricity from fossil fuel and nuclear power plants. Many people believe that wind turbines should be part of the solution to a healthier environment, not part of the problem.

Reports of Bird Deaths Are Appearing

Over the past fifteen years, a number of reports have appeared in the popular press about wind turbines killing birds. Some writers have gone so far as to dub wind generators "raptor-matics" and "cuisinarts of the sky". Unfortunately, some of these articles have been used as "evidence" to stop the construction of a wind generator in someone's back yard. The reports of dead birds create a dilemma. Do wind generators really kill birds? If so, how serious is the problem?

A confused public oftentimes does not know what to believe. Many people participate in the U.S.'s second largest pastime, bird watching. Others are truly concerned about the environment and what they perceive as yet another assault on our fragile ecosystem. Unwittingly, they rally behind the few ill-informed obstructionists who have realized that the perception of bird mortality due to wind turbines is a hot button issue, with the power to bring construction to a halt.

Birds live a tenuous existence. There are any number of things that can cause their individual deaths or collective demise. For example, bird collisions with objects in nature are a rather common occurrence, and young birds are quite clumsy when it comes to landing on a perch after flight. As a result, about 30% of total first-year bird deaths are attributed to natural collisions.

By far, the largest causes of mortality among birds include loss of habitat due to human infringement, environmental despoliation, and collisions with man-made objects. Since wind turbines fall into the last category, it is worthwhile to examine other human causes of avian deaths and compare these to mortality from wind turbines.

The Leading Causes of Bird Deaths

Utility transmission and distribution lines, the backbone of our electrical power system, are responsible for 130 to 174 million bird deaths a year in the U.S. Many of the affected birds are those with large wingspans, including raptors and waterfowl. While attempting to land on power lines and poles, birds are sometimes electrocuted when their wings span between two hot wires. Many other birds are killed as their flight paths intersect the power lines strung between poles and towers. One report states that: "for some types of birds, power line collisions appear to be a significant source of mortality."

Collisions with automobiles and trucks result in the deaths of between 60 and 80 million birds annually in the U.S. As more vehicles share the roadway, and our automotive society becomes more pervasive, these numbers will only increase. Our dependence on oil has taken its toll on birds too. Even the relatively high incidence of bird kills at Altamont Pass [California, site of

Birds such as eagles (inset) have died from electrocution and collisions with utility power lines.

wind turbines] pales in comparison to the number of birds killed from the *Exxon Valdez* oil spill in Alaska. In fact, according to author Paul Gipe, the Altamont Pass wind farm would have to operate for 500 to 1000 years to "achieve" the same mortality level as the *Exxon Valdez* event in 1989.

Tall buildings and residential house windows also claim their share of birds. Some of the five million tall buildings in U.S. cities have been documented as being a chronic mortality problem for migrating birds. There are more than 100 million houses in the U.S. House windows are more of a problem for birds in rural areas than in cities or towns. While there are no required ongoing studies of bird mortality due to buildings or house windows, the best estimates put the toll due to collisions with these structures at between 100 million and a staggering 1 billion deaths annually.

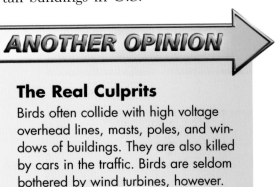

The Real Culprits

Birds often collide with high voltage overhead lines, masts, poles, and windows of buildings. They are also killed by cars in the traffic. Birds are seldom bothered by wind turbines, however.

Danish Wind Industry Association. http://www.wind power.org.

Lighted communication towers turn out to be one of the more serious problems for birds, especially for migratory species that fly at night. One study began its conclusion with, "It is apparent from the analysis of the data that significant numbers of birds are dying in collisions with communications towers, their guy wires, and related structures." Another report states, "The main environmental problem we are watching out for with telecommunication towers is the deaths of birds and bats."

This is not news, as bird collisions with lighted television and radio towers have been documented for over 50 years. Some towers are responsible for very high episodic fatalities. One television transmitter tower in Eau Claire, WI, was responsible for the deaths of over 1,000 birds on each of 24 consecutive nights. A "record 30,000 birds were estimated killed on one night" at this same tower. In Kansas, 10,000 birds were killed in one night by a telecommunications tower. Numerous large bird kills, while not as dramatic as the examples cited above, continue to occur across the country at telecommunication tower sites.

How the Causes of Bird Deaths Compare

Utility transmission and distribution lines cause the deaths of 130 to 174 million birds each year.

Automobiles and trucks cause 60 to 80 million bird deaths each year.

Tall buildings and residential house windows cause 1 billion bird deaths each year.

Wind turbines cause 6,400 deaths each year.

Source: Mick Sagrillo, "Putting Wind Power's Effect on Birds in Perspective," www.awea.org.

The number of telecommunication towers in the U.S. currently exceeds 77,000, and this number could easily double by 2010. The rush to construction is being driven mainly by our use of cell phones, and to a lesser extent by the impending switch to digital television and radio. Current mortality estimates due to telecommunication towers are 40 to 50 million birds per year. The proliferation of these towers in the near future will only exacerbate this situation.

Agricultural pesticides are "conservatively estimated" to directly kill 67 million birds per year. These numbers do not account for avian mortality associated with other pesticide applications, such as on golf courses. Nor do they take into consideration secondary losses due to pesticide use as these toxic chemicals travel up the food chain. This includes poisoning due to birds ingesting sprayed insects, the intended target of the pesticides.

Cats, both feral and housecats, also take their toll on birds. A Wisconsin Department of Natural Resources (DNR) report states that, "recent research suggests that rural free-ranging domestic cats in Wisconsin may be killing between 8 and 217 million birds each year. The most reasonable estimates indicate that 39 million birds are killed in the state each year."

There are other studies on the impacts of jet engines, smoke stacks, bridges, and any number of other human structures and activities that threaten birds on a daily basis. Together, human infrastructure and industrial activities are responsible for one to four million bird deaths per day!

Studies Show That Wind Turbines Are Not a Problem

Since the mid-1980's, a number of research organizations, universities, and consultants have conducted studies on avian mortality due to wind turbines. In the U.S., these studies were prompted because of the relatively high number of raptors that were found dead at the Altamont Pass Wind Farms near San Francisco.

After dozens of studies spanning nearly two decades, we now know that the Altamont Pass situation is unusual in the U.S.

A cat carries a wild bird in its mouth. Domestic and feral cats kill millions of birds each year.

The high raptor mortality there was the result of a convergence of factors, some of which were due to the bad siting in the local ecosystem while others were due to the wind turbine and tower technology used at the time. In fact, a very different situation exists not far away at the San Gorgonio Pass Wind Farms near Palm Springs. A 1986 study found that 69 million birds flew though the San Gorgonio Pass during the Spring and Fall migrations. During both migrating seasons, only 38 dead birds were found during that typical year, representing only 0.00006% of the migrating population.

A report recently prepared for the Bonneville Power Administration in the Northwest U.S. states that "raptor mortality has been absent to very low at all newer generation wind plants studied in the U.S. This and other information regarding wind turbine design and wind plant/wind turbine siting strongly suggests that the level of raptor mortality observed at Altamont Pass is quite unique."

The National Wind Coordinating Committee (NWCC) completed a comparison of wind farm avian mortality with bird mortality caused by other man-made structures in the U.S.

The NWCC did not conduct its own study, but analyzed all of the research done to date on various causes of avian mortality, including commercial wind farm turbines. They report that "data collected outside California indicate an average of 1.83 avian fatalities per turbine (for all species combined), and 0.006 raptor fatalities per turbine per year. Based on current projections of 3,500 operational wind turbines in the US by the end of 2001, excluding California, the total annual mortality was estimated at approximately 6,400 bird fatalities per year for all species combined."

This report states that its intent is to "put avian mortality associated with windpower development into perspective with other significant sources of avian collision mortality across the United States." The NWCC reports that: "Based on current estimates, windplant related avian collision fatalities probably represent from 0.01% to 0.02% (i.e., 1 out of every 5,000 to 10,000) of the annual avian collision fatalities in the United States." That is, commercial wind turbines cause the direct deaths of only 0.01% to 0.02% of all of the birds killed by collisions with man-made structures and activities in the U.S.

A Wisconsin Study Shows That Wind Turbines' Impact on Birds Is Insignificant

My home state of Wisconsin is a good example of current research. In December of 2002, the report "Effects of Wind Turbines on Birds and Bats in Northeast Wisconsin" was released. The study was completed by Robert Howe and Amy Wolf of the University of Wisconsin-Green Bay, and William

Evans. Their study covered a two-year period between 1999 and 2001, in the area surrounding the 31 turbines operating in Kewaunee County by Madison Gas & Electric (MG&E) and Wisconsin Public Service (WPS) Corporation.

The report found that over the study period, 25 bird carcasses were found at the sites. The report states that "the resulting mortality rate of 1.29 birds/tower/year is close to the nationwide estimate of 2.19 birds/tower." The report further states, "While bird collisions do occur (with commercial wind turbines) the impacts on global populations appear to be relatively minor, especially in comparison with other human-related causes of mortality such as communications towers, collisions with buildings, and vehicles collisions. This is especially true for small scale facilities like the MG&E and WPS wind farms in Kewaunee County."

The report goes on to say, "previous studies suggest that the frequency of avian collisions with wind turbines is low, and the impact of wind power on bird populations today is negligible. Our study provides little evidence to refute this claim."

So, while wind farms are responsible for the deaths of some birds, when put into the perspective of other causes of avian mortality, the impact is quite low. In other words, bird mortality at wind farms, compared to other human-related causes of bird mortality, is biologically and statistically insignificant. There is no evidence that birds are routinely being battered out of the air by rotating wind turbine blades as postulated by some in the popular press.

Home-Sized Wind Systems Are Not a Problem Either

How does all of this impact the homeowner who wishes to secure a building permit to install a wind generator and tower on his or her property? They will likely still be quizzed by zoning officials or a concerned public with little to go on but the sensational headlines in the regional press. But while the press may or may not get the facts right, people's concerns are real, and need to be addressed with factual information such as is presented here.

While there have been any number of studies done on bird mortality caused by commercial wind installations, none have been done on the impact of home-sized wind systems on birds. The reason? It is just not an issue, especially when "big" wind's impact on birds is considered biologically insignificant.

When confronted with the question of why there were no studies done on home-sized wind systems and birds, a Wisconsin Department of Natural Resources person familiar with these issues responded, "It is not even on the radar screen."

Wind turbines, described by some as posing little danger to birds, spin at a wind farm near Palm Springs, California.

There has never been a report or documentation of a home-sized wind turbine killing birds in Wisconsin.

The Wisconsin Department of Natural Resources, or any other government or research organization for that matter, just does not have the financial resources to conduct a study just because a zoning official requests it, especially given the lack of evidence nationwide that any problem exists with home-sized turbines. Based on our best available information, the relatively smaller blades and short tower heights of residential wind energy systems do not present a threat to birds.

References

John S. Coleman, Stanley A. Temple, and Scott R. Craven, "Cats and Wildlife: A Conservation Dilemma," University of Wisconsin-Extension, 1997.

Joe Eaton, "Tower Kill," *Earth Island Journal,* Winter 2003.

Robert W. Howe, William Evans, and Amy T. Wolf, "Effects of Wind Turbines on Birds and Bats in Northeast Wisconsin," November 2002.

Cat Laazaroff, "Communication Tower Guidelines Could Protect Migrating Birds," Environmental News Service, 2002.

National Wind Coordinating Committee, "Avian Collisions with Wind Turbines: A Summary of Existing Studies and Comparisons to Other Sources of Avian Collision Mortality in the United States," West, Inc., August 2001.

David Pimentel and H. Acquay, "The Environmental and Economic Costs of Pesticide," *Bioscience,* November 1992.

Gavin G. Shire, Karen Brown, and Gerald Winegrad, "Communication Towers: A Deadly Hazard To Birds," American Bird Conservancy, June 2000.

"Synthesis and Comparison of Baseline Avian and Bat Use, Raptor Nesting and Mortality Information from Proposed and Existing Wind Developments," West, Inc., December 2002.

Wendy K. Weisenel, "Battered By Airwaves," Wisconsin Department of Natural Resources, October 2002.

A Cape Cod Wind Farm Would Harm the Environment

Robert F. Kennedy Jr.

While many Americans support wind power in the abstract, they often protest when a real wind farm is slated to be built near them. This phenomenon can be seen in the intense debate over the proposal to build a wind farm in Nantucket Sound off Cape Cod. While many environmentalists support the project, others—often those who live nearby—claim it will destroy wildlife and harm the region's tourism and fishing industries. Controversies over the siting of wind farms are especially contentious when the proposed location is along a coastline, where turbines would mar the view.

In the following selection Robert F. Kennedy Jr. weighs in on this debate. He agrees with those against the wind farm, contending that it would destroy a national treasure. Kennedy also claims that wilderness areas such as Nantucket Sound that are located near urban centers are especially valuable and should be protected. According to him, advances in turbine technology will soon enable companies to erect wind farms farther from shore, thereby eliminating many of the problems associated with the Cape Wind project. Robert F. Kennedy Jr. is an environmental lawyer and professor at Pace University Law School in New York.

As an environmentalist, I support wind power, including wind power on the high seas. I am also involved in siting wind farms in appropriate landscapes, of which there are many. But I do believe that some places should be off limits to any sort of industrial development. I wouldn't build a wind farm in Yosemite National Park. Nor would I build one on Nantucket Sound, which is exactly what the company Energy Management is trying to do with its Cape Wind project.

This is a view of Cape Cod from outer space. A proposed wind farm off the Cape is a source of intense debate.

Environmental groups have been enticed by Cape Wind, but they should be wary of lending support to energy companies that are trying to privatize the commons—in this case 24 square miles of a heavily used waterway. And because offshore wind costs twice as much as gas-fired electricity and significantly more than onshore wind, the project is financially feasible only because the federal and state governments have promised $241 million in subsidies.

The Environmental Hazards Associated with Cape Wind

Cape Wind's proposal involves construction of 130 giant turbines whose windmill arms will reach 417 feet above the water and be visible for up to 26 miles. These turbines are less than six miles from shore and would be seen from Cape Cod, Martha's Vineyard and Nantucket. Hundreds of flashing lights to warn airplanes away from the turbines will steal the stars and nighttime views. The noise of the turbines will be audible onshore. A transformer substation rising 100 feet above the sound would house giant helicopter pads and 40,000 gallons of potentially hazardous oil.

According to the Massachusetts Historical Commission, the project will damage the views from 16 historic sites and lighthouses on the cape and nearby islands. The Humane Society estimates the whirling turbines could every year kill thousands of migrating songbirds and sea ducks.

Cape Wind Will Harm Local Industries

Nantucket Sound is among the most densely traveled boating corridors in the Atlantic. The turbines will be perilously close to the main navigation channels for cargo ships, ferries and fishing boats. The risk of collisions with the towers would increase during the fogs and storms for which the area is famous. That is why the Steamship Authority and Hy-Line Cruises, which transport millions of passengers to and from the cape and islands every year, oppose the project. Thousands of small businesses, including marina owners, hotels, motels, whale watching tours and charter fishing operations will also be hurt. The Beacon Hill Institute at Suffolk University in Boston estimates a loss of up to 2,533 jobs because of the loss of tourism—and over a billion dollars to the local economy.

Nantucket Sound is a critical fishing ground for the commercial fishing families of Martha's Vineyard and Cape Cod. Hundreds of fishermen work Horseshoe Shoal, where the Cape Wind project would be built, and make half their annual income from the catch. The risks that their gear will become fouled in the spider web of cables between the 130 towers will largely preclude fishing in the area, destroying family-owned businesses that enrich the palate, economy and culture of Cape Cod.

Many environmental groups support the Cape Wind project, and that's unfortunate because making enemies of fishermen and marina owners is bad environmental strategy in the long run. Cape Cod's traditional-gear commercial fishing families and its recreational anglers and marina owners have all been important allies for environmentalists in our battles for clean water.

Cape Cod's Marvels Need to Be Protected

There are those who argue that unlike our great Western national parks, Cape Cod is far from pristine, and that Cape Wind's turbines won't be a significant blot. I invite these critics to see the pods of humpback, minke, pilot, finback and right whales off Nantucket, [and] to marvel at the thousands of harbor and gray seals lolling on the bars off Monomoy and Horseshoe Shoal. . . .

I urge them to come diving on some of the hundreds of historic wrecks in this "graveyard of the Atlantic," and to visit the endless dune-covered beaches of Cape Cod, our fishing villages immersed in history and beauty, or to spend an afternoon netting blue crabs or mucking clams, quahogs and scallops by the bushel on tidal mud flats—some of the reasons my uncle, John F. Kennedy, authorized the creation of the Cape Cod National Seashore in 1961, and why Nantucket Sound is under consideration as a national marine sanctuary, a designation that would prohibit commercial electrical generation.

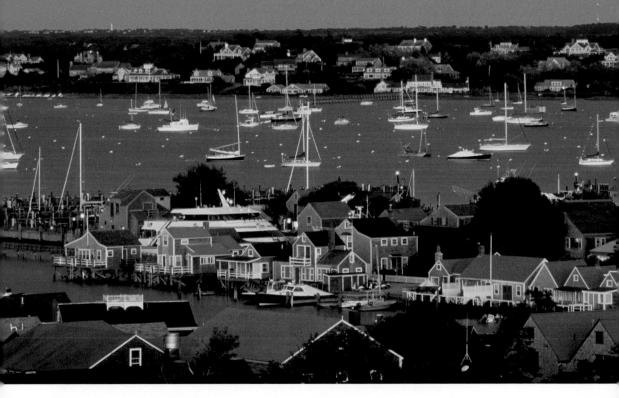

Opponents of wind farms worry about marring the beauty of Nantucket (pictured), where many wealthy people have summer homes.

All of us need periodically to experience wilderness to renew our spirits and reconnect ourselves to the common history of our nation, humanity and to God. The worst trap that environmentalists can fall into is the conviction that the only wilderness worth preserving is in the Rocky Mountains or Alaska. To the contrary, our most important wildernesses are those that are closest to our densest population centers, like Nantucket Sound.

Situating Turbines in Deeper Water Would Be Better

There are many alternatives that would achieve the same benefits as Cape Wind without destroying this national treasure. Deep water technology is rapidly evolving, promising huge bounties of wind energy with fewer environmental and

Possible Developments in Wind Turbine Technology

This diagram shows how improvements in wind technology will enable engineers to locate turbines in increasingly deep water.

| **Current Technology** | **Shallow Water** | **Transitional Depths** | **Deep Water** |
| Offshore wind turbine | 0 to 30 meters | 30 to 50 meters | 50 to 200 meters |

Source: National Renewable Energy Laboratory, June, 2004. www.nrel.gov.

economic consequences. Scotland is preparing to build wind turbines in the Moray Firth more than 12 miles offshore. Germany is considering placing turbines as far as 27 miles off its northern shores.

If Cape Wind were to place its project further offshore, it could build not just 130, but thousands of windmills—where they can make a real difference in the battle against global warming without endangering the birds or impoverishing the experience of millions of tourists and residents and fishing families who rely on the sound's unspoiled bounties.

A Cape Cod Wind Farm Would Benefit the Environment

Cape Wind

Cape Wind, developed by Energy Management Inc., is proposing America's first offshore wind farm on Horseshoe Shoal in Nantucket Sound off Cape Cod. The project has become the center of intense debate. Many environmentalists say that the project will expand the use of environmentally friendly wind power. Other environmentalists—especially those who live or summer near the sound—claim that the project will mar views and damage the local environment.

In the following selection Cape Wind responds to environmental lawyer Robert F. Kennedy Jr.'s concerns about its proposed wind farm. Kennedy claims that the farm will harm the local environment. On the contrary, Cape Wind contends, building more wind farms will cut down on America's use of polluting fossil fuels, which contributes to global warming. Cape Wind also counters Kennedy's assertion that the wind farm will mar views. The organization points out that the turbines, located 6 miles (9.6km) out to sea, barely will be seen from shore. Moreover, while Kennedy maintains that the wind farm should be located farther out to sea once technological advances make turbines more seaworthy, Cape Wind argues that action against global warming must be taken now.

Editor's Note: Extracts from Robert F. Kennedy Jr.'s editorial in the *New York Times* appear in italics. Cape Wind's responses to Kennedy's comments appear in normal text.

"The future of wind energy depends on the offshore market."
—Arthourus Zervos, President, European Wind Energy Association http://www.planetark.com.

*A*s an environmentalist, I support wind power, including wind power on the high seas. I am also involved in siting wind farms in appropriate landscapes, of which there are many. But I do believe that some places should be off limits to any sort of industrial development. I wouldn't build a wind farm in Yosemite National Park. Nor would I build one on Nantucket Sound . . .

Author and environmentalist Charles Komanoff considered this objection by [Robert F. Kennedy] Jr. to Cape Wind when he wrote:

"If anyone should understand the need to maximize the energy output from wind turbines, it is environmentalists—particularly those who live or summer on Cape Cod. In the coming decades, Cape beaches will be inundated and Cape dunes and structures battered by rising sea levels and increasingly violent storms, wrought by global warming. And, sure as daylight, continued reliance on oil will not only contaminate the environment but also fuel the cycle of war and terrorism.

"Yet somehow [some] environmental groups and high-profile individuals such as [Robert F.] Kennedy [Jr.] can't connect the dots. They decry the April [2004] breakup of a barge carrying bunker oil to a Cape electricity-generating plant that has shut a prized shellfishing area and many beaches. But they can't see that stopping Cape Wind will subject Buzzards Bay to such oil shipments for decades. Nor does it seem to matter to them that other precious—albeit less prosperous—places, from West Virginia mountaintops to Wyoming sandhills, are sacrificed daily to yield the very fuels that the wind farm would displace.

"If obstructionists such as Kennedy and the Alliance to Protect Nantucket Sound have their way, wind power may never amount to more than a 'niche' energy source. What is at present our most promising large-scale energy alternative—and certainly the most alluring—could be strangled in its cradle as the NIMBY [Not In My Back Yard] precedent takes hold nationwide.

"History's great movements have all been universal, not selective. Abolitionists fought to free all slaves, not some. Labor sought to organize all workers, not just the most skilled. Environmentalists from John Muir to Rachel Carson campaigned to save nature everywhere—not just in a few 'unique' areas.

"It remains to be seen whether latter-day environmentalism will rouse itself to protect the whole earth—or degenerate into a protection scheme for the pretty views of well-to-do landowners."

Environmental groups have been enticed by Cape Wind, but they should be wary of lending support to energy companies that are trying to privatize the commons

Cape Wind president Jim Gordon gives an update on the progress of Cape Wind's plans.

There is a long history in the United States of commercial activities being permitted on public lands when they are found to serve the public interest. In the case of clean, renewable energy, State and Federal policies clearly recognize the public interest benefits of cleaner air, job creation, greater electric price stability and reduced dependence on imported energy. It has also been noted by the US Department of Energy that because New England is so heavily dependent on natural gas for electric generation the region is at risk of esca-

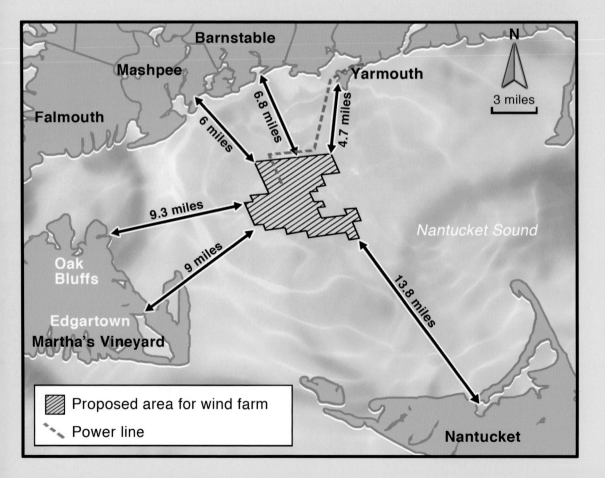

The Proposed Area for the Cape Cod Wind Farm

lating prices and even winter rolling blackouts due to fuel shortages and that Cape Wind would provide regional electric reliability benefits.

Ultimately, Cape Wind will only receive its permits if government agencies determine the project is consistent with the public interest. Opponents of Cape Wind have consistently favored moves to prevent the permitting process from moving forward and to prevent the public interest determination of the project from ever being made.

in this case 24 square miles of a heavily used waterway

Nantucket Sound is over 500 square miles in size. While it is true that the Horseshoe Shoal area where the wind turbines would be located is 24 square miles, the wind turbines themselves would occupy less than one tenth of one percent of that shoal area. There would be 6 to 9 football fields of separation between the wind turbines to allow considerable room to navigate for the shallow draft vessels that go onto the shallow shoal. . . .

Cape Wind's proposal involves construction of 130 giant turbines whose windmill arms will reach 417 feet above the water and be visible for up to 26 miles

In clear conditions, from a distance of 6 miles at the shoreline of Hyannis Port, the wind turbines will appear one half inch high on the horizon if you were to extend your arm straight in front of you and separated your thumb and index finger. From the Town of Nantucket, at 13.8 miles, the wind turbines would appear as tiny specks on the horizon in clear conditions.

. . . lights to warn airplanes away from the turbines will steal the stars and nighttime views

Though navigation safety lights will be visible from shore at night, they will not appear bright and they will not appreciably affect the visibility of stars overhead.

The noise of the turbines will be audible onshore

The operation of the wind turbines six miles offshore will never be audible from shore. Visitors to existing offshore wind turbines in Europe consistently report that the wind turbines are difficult to even hear up close, from a nearby boat. Wind turbine noise has been substantially reduced with improvements in the technology over the years and the background sounds offshore of wind and surf are also considerable.

A transformer substation rising 100 feet above the sound would house giant helicopter pads and 40,000 gallons of potentially hazardous oil

The reference here is to highly refined mineral oil that will be far more secure than the millions of gallons of fuel oils that traverse Nantucket Sound every year. The mineral oil will be stored in a triple-containment system to protect against any spills.

In addition, Cape Wind will reduce the amount of fossil fuels, including oil, that is burned in New England to make electricity. Each year Cape Wind will generate as much electricity as it would take an oil burning power plant burning 113 million gallons of oil to produce. Cape Wind has earned the support of the highly-respected Coalition For Buzzards Bay in part due to their analysis that Cape Wind would reduce the risk of oil spills like the 100,000 gallons of oil spilled into Buzzards Bay in 2003 that was en route to an oil burning power plant located onshore the Cape Cod Canal. That spill resulted in the deaths of over 450 seabirds, befouled beaches and closed shellfish beds for over a year.

According to the Massachusetts Historical Commission, the project will damage the views from 16 historic sites and lighthouses on the cape and nearby islands

Although the Massachusetts Historical Commission did find that the project would have an "adverse effect" on the views of some historic sites including the Kennedy Compound (that incidentally has no public access), the methodology they used to reach that determination was whether the new view would be consistent with the historic view. As there have never before been offshore wind turbines in Nantucket Sound, it was fairly certain they would reach this particular determination.

Wind power is hardly a new concept for Cape Cod and the Islands, however. In the late 1700s and early 1800s there were up to a thousand working windmills on Cape Cod and the Islands of Martha's Vineyard and Nantucket. The windmills were helping make salt, pump water and grind grain—the wind powered the local economy. The remaining windmills are treasured tourist attractions and are an icon of the cultural history of Cape Cod and the Islands.

This lighthouse in Nantucket Harbor is part of the charm of Cape Cod.

The Humane Society estimates the whirling turbines could every year kill thousands of migrating songbirds and sea ducks

Extensive studies of operational offshore wind farms in Europe in areas with lots of birds have found very few bird collisions; most birds are found to avoid the wind farms and those that fly through tend to travel down the open corridors between turbine rows.

It is important to also consider that conventional energy uses pose very high risks to birds from oil spills to habitat loss caused by energy extraction and acid rain, from mercury contamination and from arguably the biggest threat—global warming.

The Humane Society calculations ignored the studied experience of offshore wind farms in Europe and their work has been financed, in part, by the opposition group that formed to stop the Cape Wind project. . . .

All of us need periodically to experience wilderness to renew our spirits and reconnect ourselves to the common history of our nation, humanity and to God. The worst trap that environmentalists can fall into is the conviction that the only wilderness worth preserving is in the Rocky Mountains or Alaska. To the contrary, our most important wildernesses are those that are closest to our densest population centers, like Nantucket Sound.

Wind turbines stand in the deep waters of the Irish Sea at an offshore wind farm. U.S. offshore wind turbines may be years away.

Dense population centers are also the areas of highest electricity demand. Local, clean and natural energy can meet an increasing share of this demand from sources like offshore wind.

There are many alternatives that would achieve the same benefits as Cape Wind without destroying this national treasure. Deep water technology is rapidly evolving, promising huge bounties of wind energy with fewer environmental and economic consequences. Scotland is preparing to build wind turbines in the Moray Firth more than 12 miles offshore. Germany is considering placing turbines as far as 27 miles off its northern shores

The Moray Firth project is a heavily subsidized demonstration project that will power existing offshore oil rigs—the electricity will not be cabled to shore. The developers of the project think commercial applications of their research and development are 10 to 15 years away.

The US Department of Energy also estimates that deepwater offshore wind farms, further from shore, are 10–15 years away and they acknowledge the important and beneficial role that shallow water projects closer to shore can play now to help usher in this important energy supply. . . .

If Cape Wind were to place its project further offshore, it could build not just 130, but thousands of windmills—where they can make a real difference in the battle against global warming

Cape Wind will make a meaningful contribution to the efforts in the region to reduce carbon dioxide . . . emissions that cause global warming. Natural Resources Defense Council has noted that Cape Wind "is, to our knowledge, the largest single source of supply-side reductions in CO_2 [carbon dioxide] currently proposed in the United States, and perhaps in the world." Cape Wind will also help to usher in technology that will allow for deeper water wind turbine installations, in higher wave environments to make possible the thousands of offshore wind turbines Robert F. Kennedy Jr. envisions to be built sooner, rather than later.

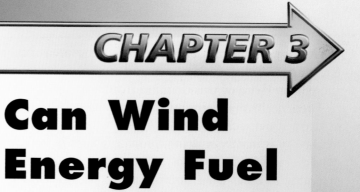

CHAPTER 3

Can Wind Energy Fuel the Future?

An engineer stands inside the doorway of a wind turbine in England.

Wind Energy Can Meet America's Future Energy Needs

John Dunlop and Mike Sloan, interviewed by Ira Flatow

Wind power contributes less than 1 percent of the United States's energy, but many experts believe it can become a more significant energy source in the future. The following selection presents the views of two representatives of the wind energy industry who argue that wind energy has enormous potential. Appearing on the National Public Radio program *Talk of the Nation: Science Friday*, hosted by science journalist Ira Flatow, John Dunlop and Mike Sloan explain how wind energy is helping America meet its energy needs. Dunlop says the American Wind Energy Association's members aim to supply 6 percent of the nation's electricity by 2020, and much more beyond that. Sloan points out that wind energy could become a new source of revenue for farmers and ranchers who erect wind turbines on their land. Both Dunlop and Sloan conclude that wind power will become a significant energy source in the United States. John Dunlop is the Northern Great Plains regional manager for the American Wind Energy Association. Mike Sloan is head of the Texas Wind Energy Coalition and president of an energy consulting firm.

Ira Flatow, "Talk of the Nation: Science Friday (Analysis: Wind Power)," *National Public Radio*, June 20, 2003. Reproduced by permission.

Ira Flatow: This hour, we'll be talking and taking a look at what seems to be the perfect energy source. It's clean. It's non-polluting. It's renewable. Nobody owns it: the wind. Wind energy currently powers, oh, a little over a million households in the US. And, of course, that's just a tiny amount. But it's also just a fraction of the estimated wind power that can be harnessed. But the numbers are also on the rise. Right now, California, Texas and Iowa are the leaders in wind production. But new laws in Minnesota could put that state in the number-one spot by the year 2012. In fact, Minnesota is expected to increase its wind capacity by tenfold in the next 10 years. Wind power is very big in Europe, of course. A third of the electric power of Denmark, for example, comes from the wind.

In Minnesota, which has seen gains in wind production, workers raise the blades of a wind turbine.

So what are the obstacles to harnessing the wind? Do you have to live in a windy place? What kinds of changes in our energy production and distribution systems would need to happen before we'll all start seeing turbines? Oh, yes, they're called turbines now. Don't call these things windmills. . . . These are big, sleek machines, some as high as a 20-story building. And they can produce, oh, one and a half megawatts of power, each one of them, enough to supply about 300 houses. And even bigger wind turbines are on the drawing board. . . .

Let me introduce my guests. John Dunlop is the Northern Great Plains regional manager of the American Wind Energy Association. And that regional office is in Minneapolis. And he joins us today from Wisconsin Public Radio in central Wisconsin, where he is attending the Midwest Renewable Energy Fair.

Thanks for taking time to talk with us today, Mr. Dunlop.

John Dunlop: It's a great pleasure.

You're welcome. Also with us is Mike Sloan. He's the president of Virtus Energy Research Associates in Austin, Texas. He's also the executive director of the Texas Wind Coalition, and he joins us by phone.

Thanks for talking with us today, Mr. Sloan.

Mike Sloan: It's a pleasure to be here.

John, how much of a potential is there for wind energy in this country?

The Potential of Wind Is Enormous

Dunlop: One of the nice things about wind energy is that it is very intense. A number of our states can produce many times more electricity than we currently produce, than we currently use in the respective states. And so the potential is absolutely enormous. Our association would aspire to achieve 6 percent of our entire nation's electricity coming from wind power by 2020.

And what is the potential for—if you go, you know, down the road? Could you make it a lot more than that?

Dunlop: Oh, the potential is many times more than that.

I've seen estimates that there's enough wind power, if we harnessed all the wind here, to be twice the amount of electricity that we're using now. We could take care of all of it.

Dunlop: It's at least that, Ira. It looks like we can produce about 2,700 terawatt hours or 2,700 billion kilowatt hours.

Mike Sloan, I'm looking at a map of the country put out by the National Renewable Energy Lab in Golden, Colorado. It's a federal research—I'm sure you're familiar with it. And it shows all the installed bases of wind power in the country. And I was very surprised to see that Texas ranks second to California. Texas—25 percent of all the wind power installed in the country comes from Texas. Why is that?

Texas Produces Much Wind Energy

Sloan: Well, when Texas decides to get involved in something, they usually like to do it in a big way, and that's exactly what's happened with wind power. One of the reasons is that it is so cost-effective here. Even though we're a very big state and we have a lot of low-cost oil and coal and natural gas, the wind power, because of the really great winds we have out in west Texas, are also very, very cost competitive now in the Texas market. So it really came on very, very quickly.

Give me an idea of the economics there. If I wanted to put a wind turbine on my ranch, how does that work? Give me a thumbnail sketch of how that would work.

Sloan: Well, there's two ways to go, and I'm speaking now globally, all over the world. In the United States, typically, they're developed by large power companies, and they might put 50 to even, say, 200 of these wind turbines in a big development that's commonly called a wind farm. But each wind turbine costs about $1 million, the very large 20-story tall ones that you referred to before. So not every rancher and farmer has $200 million in his back pocket, so they leave that to the big energy companies. Now if an individual rancher or a farmer wanted to put up one, sometimes they get together in little co-ops and do it; and actually, that's the type of development that we don't have much of in Texas, but they have a little bit going on up in Minnesota. So here in Texas, very big energy projects, and they've resulted in very competitive cost of electricity.

And, of course, Texans are used to having oil rigs and things in their back yards. Why not a wind turbine?

Sloan: Exactly. It's really striking. If you're ever flying over Texas out West, and when you get around Midland in the middle of the oil patch, and you look out the window down there, you can see the wind farms and the oil fields right next to each other, and it's dramatic how similar they are. You've got a wind

Utility power transmission lines may one day carry more electricity from wind generators than from nuclear power plants.

turbine or an oil well, and they're going to be spaced out very similarly and they'll have roads connecting them, but you'll still see the cattle running around all of them and doing the normal things that we've done in west Texas before we had wind or even before we had oil.

So how much does a rancher get for having a turbine on his property?

Sloan: What's typical is about $2,000 per turbine, and we've got one rancher out in west Texas who has about 200 of them on his property, and just working that math, 200 turbines times $2,000 a year, you can imagine that that rancher likes wind quite a bit.

U.S. Wind Energy, in Megawatts

WA 243.8
OR 259.4
ID 0.2
MT 0.1
WY 284.6
ND 66.3
SD 44.3
NE 14.0
MN 562.7
IA 471.2
WI 53.0
MI 2.4
IL 50.4
OH 3.6
PA 129.0
NY 48.5
VT 6.0
ME 0.1
NH 0.1
MA 1.0
CA 2,042.6
UT 0.2
CO 223.2
KS 113.7
WV 66.0
NM 206.6
OK 176.3
AR 0.1
TN 2.0
AK 1.1
TX 1,293.0
HI 8.6

Source: "2003 U.S. Wind Capacity Map," in *Wind Power Today and Tomorrow*, U.S. Department of Energy, National Renewable Energy Laboratory, National Wind Technology Center, 2004. www.nrel.gov/.

He's making $400,000, is that about it?

Sloan: That's about right.

And does he have to give up his cattle for that or. . . .

Sloan: Not at all. In fact, if you look at it and just work it out on a per acre basis, there's not a lot of water in west Texas, so you need a lot of land to run cattle, and just your gross income you're going to see from cattle operations in west Texas is about $5 per acre. And working out the math on the wind turbine, they're going to make a profit of $50 per acre. So you can imagine they really like wind out in west Texas.

I'll bet.

Minnesota Is Becoming a Leader in Wind Power

John Dunlop, Mike mentioned Minnesota. Tell us a little bit about what's happening in Minnesota.

Dunlop: Minnesota actually had the pleasure of leading—as we like to say up here—leading the entire nation in wind energy development during the 1990s. That was until Texas came along in the late '90s. But during that time, there were numerous laws that were passed in Minnesota in the early part of the decade that led to a leadership position. And actually, Minnesota was number two in the nation until it was superseded by Texas, and then last year [2002], as you mentioned, by Iowa. However, this year, as you mentioned, Ira, the Minnesota Legislature dealt with some issues with regard to the storage of nuclear waste. And as a part of that package, we have adopted measures in Minnesota that will, as you say, thrust Minnesota back into a leadership position nationally in terms of new wind energy development.

Not only will the laws stimulate the large utility scale projects, but they will also provide an incentive and actually a requirement to acquire the small utility type turbines, less than two megawatts of capacity, that Mike was talking about. We currently have about 80 megawatts of the small dispersed projects installed, and the new legislation would increase that capacity by about threefold.

Hmm. And there are bigger wind turbines on the block, on the drawing board, correct?

These farmers in Minnesota earn extra income by renting out space for wind turbines on their land.

Dunlop: The typical wind turbine that is going in today in the region is the 1.5 megawatt size or class of turbine. They're, as you mentioned, quite enormous. Typically, they're about between 70 and 80 meters in diameter, so that's well over three-quarters of a football field in diameter, sitting on towers that are over two-thirds of a football field directly up in the air.

And how do you get the—let me ask both of you gentlemen. When the electricity comes out, is it made to power the local homes or do you feed it to the [power] grid? And, John, why don't you answer that first.

Wind Power Gets Directed to Consumers Everywhere

Dunlop: The electricity—our entire electric system in the entire—well, not quite the entire United States. There's an Eastern grid and a Western grid and then, of course, as Mike will quickly point out, there's a Texas grid. But regardless if you're in one of those grids, all of the utilities are interconnected together. And so the utilities balance the amount of electricity produced on an instantaneous basis to meet that load. When the wind is blowing, which is the vast majority of the time, especially if you're dispersed geographically around one of the distribution grids, the electricity is simply integrated into that system, and the utility [needs to] produce less electricity when the electricity is coming from the wind.

And in Texas, is it locally used or is it fed to the grid there, too?

Sloan: It really is fed all over the state to where people use electricity, and that was one of the, I guess, responses to the

San Antonio is one of the cities that benefits from the extra electricity generated by the windmills in Texas.

laws that we had. Back in '99, Texas restructured its electric industry, and one of the things that was important was to make sure that there was some renewable energy in the system, and the rules that they used require electric utilities all over the state to get some very small fraction, about 1/2 of 1 percent right now, from renewable energy. Wind power being the cheapest renewable, that's what most of the companies are getting. So here in Texas, what we're seeing is most of the wind power is going to the big cities, such as Dallas and Houston and San Antonio and Austin.

And is there a stumbling block toward expanding this or have you reached a capacity? What is the future here?

Sloan: Oh, in Texas, there's enormous additional amounts. We get about 1 percent of our electricity right now from wind power, and it's about 1,000 megawatts, that's total installed wind capacity on the ground. We have the potential for 500 megawatts or more, so 500 times expansion. It's virtually an unlimited resource. It is only limited by the infrastructure and our ability to get it to those cities, which means electric transmission lines to move the power.

Wind Energy Is Too Expensive

Neil Hrab

In the following selection Neil Hrab contends that wind energy is so expensive to produce that it must be funded by government subsidies in order to compete with fossil fuels. He claims that environmentalists and wind power companies are in league together to make sure that Congress continues to fund the building of wind farms. According to Hrab, subsidizing wind power forces consumers to pay more for electricity. Such subsidies might be worth the cost if the money were being used to develop more efficient turbines, he argues, but presently it is being used simply to support inefficient wind farms that generate more profit for wind companies than they do electricity. Neil Hrab is the Warren T. Brookes fellow at the Competitive Enterprise Institute, a nonprofit public policy organization dedicated to advancing the principles of free enterprise and limited government.

Have you ever heard of Baptists allying themselves with bootleggers? It actually happened in the early 20th century, when temperance activists in parts of the South struck political bargains with moonshiners and alcohol smugglers. The temperance activists, guided by their religious beliefs, wanted to reduce the number of legal opportunities for consumers to buy liquor. (This campaign culminated in what we remember as Prohibition.) These activists' arguments provided cover for their bootlegging brethren, who wanted to limit those opportunities to purchase booze as well—but not for religious reasons. The bootleggers supported sales

Neil Hrab, "Baptists, Bootleggers, and Wind Power," www.cei.org, March 22, 2004. Reproduced by permission of the author and the Competitive Enterprise Institute.

restrictions in order to force consumers to purchase homemade firewater, instead of the legal stuff brewed by their (legal) competitors. Fewer chances to buy alcohol legally meant higher profits for the bootleggers, who would become the vendor of last resort for the South's parched throats.

This odd pairing inspired Bruce Yandle, a professor of economics at Clemson University, to coin the phrase "Baptist-bootlegger alliance." This expression refers to political bargains struck by special interest groups to advance some shared goal, usually at the expense of average consumers. The Baptists enter into the alliance for moral reasons; the bootleggers join out of practical self-interest.

The Pro-Wind Lobbyists Want Subsidies

You can observe a latter-day Baptist-bootlegger alliance by studying America's pro–wind power movement. This lobby

An old postcard from the days of Prohibition shows how common bootlegging was. Some compare wind power proponents to bootleggers.

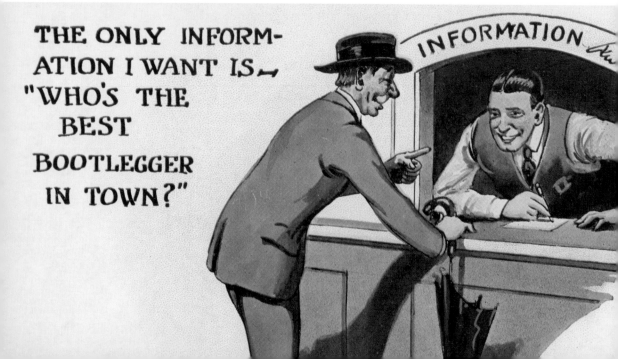

THE ONLY INFORM-
ATION I WANT IS—
"WHO'S THE
BEST
BOOTLEGGER
IN TOWN?"

INFORMATION

The Natural Resources Defense Council (NRDC), located in southern California, promotes expanded use of wind power.

wants all levels of government to give the wind power industry various forms of assistance, including subsidies and special tax treatment.

Let's get clear on how wind power works. First, you need to set up a series of massive turbines—often stretching 300 feet in height. (That's taller than the US Capitol building, which is 288 feet high.) The turbine's blades spin as the wind blows, capturing the wind's energy and using it to create electricity.

Who are the Baptists in this alliance? They are not hard to identify—most of them hail from tax-exempt environmentalist organizations. With all the faith and passion of the temperance activists of yore, greens believe the promotion of wind power will lead the United States towards a better, purer, cleaner future.

The Sierra Club backs wind power, for example, because it represents an alternative to fossil fuels. It also claims that wind

A crane lifts a wind tower rotor to the top of a wind turbine in Germany, one of many European countries that uses wind power.

power is good for rural America, because it will create jobs there. The Natural Resources Defense Council says wind power is one way to wean America off foreign supplies of oil and improve national security.

For its part, Environmental Defense thinks that the US is in danger of being left behind, technologically speaking, if it does not invest more resources in wind power. It says that the European Union annually produces "more than four times as much energy through wind as the USA, and experts predict that within 10 years at least 10 percent of Europe's electrical energy needs will be supplied by giant wind turbines hooked up to main power grids."

Many Companies Stand to Profit from Wind Power

The bootlegger side of the equation is easy to decipher. There are many companies that see wind power as a highly profitable opportunity. These companies are open about the fact that in order for wind power to really catch on, they believe it (i.e., their companies) needs a lot of grants and non-monetary forms of assistance from local, state, and federal governments. The arguments circulated by pro–wind power greens provide seemingly objective justifications and rationalizations for this special pleading by the wind power industry.

The pro–wind power movement posits that since European countries have sunk lots of money into building up their wind power capacity, the US should do the same. But some Europeans think the giveaways enjoyed by their wind power industry are wasteful. The European branch of the International Federation of Industrial Energy Consumers [IFIEC] claims in a recent paper that the subsidies given to wind power are not helping wind power become more competitive with fossil fuels—all they do is "simply guarantee revenues over an extensive period" to wind power companies with money taken from taxpayers. The subsidies sound less like a way to help the wind industry perfect its technology and more like a free taxpayer-subsidized lunch for well-connected entrepreneurs.

Europeans Pay More for Energy

The IFIEC makes one more important point. It questions whether it is fair that European companies should have to pay more for electricity thanks to the special taxes and fees governments impose to support wind power. This translates into higher energy costs for European firms. Some Europeans worry that these extra costs put their companies at a comparative disadvantage with their competitors in Asia and North America. As the IFIEC paper puts it: "For European industry it is vital not to increase the price for an essential industrial product—power—to support a single technology [i.e., wind power] otherwise far from being marketable." If European industry leaders think wind power subsidies are sapping their economic strength, maybe that means American companies should think twice before jumping on the wind power bandwagon.

As calls to increase subsidies to wind power increase in the United States, electricity consumers in this country may want to take some lessons from the European experience—especially when they read the sort of pro–wind power manifestos reviewed above. Perhaps the day will come when wind power technology becomes efficient enough that its widespread use makes sense. In light of the IFIEC report, American taxpayers should press wind power backers to show how subsidies to their industry would be used for something other than the construction of a comfortable, publicly funded financial hammock (as seems to be the case in Europe).

And if they can't, then the pro–wind power bluster spread by enviro-Baptists can be dismissed as a bunch of hot air.

Wind Will Become the World's Leading Energy Source

Lester R. Brown

At the beginning of the twenty-first century, wind power supplied a tiny fraction of the world's energy needs. In the following selection, however, environmentalist Lester R. Brown argues that wind is rapidly becoming the world's chief source of electric power. He notes that wind energy is available nearly everywhere and, unlike coal or oil, it cannot be depleted. Wind power generation is also becoming cheaper, making it competitive with other energy sources, such as coal. Furthermore, wind energy does not pollute the way that coal and oil do, Brown points out. He projects that many countries will follow the lead of Denmark and Germany, which produce a significant amount of electricity from wind. Lester R. Brown is founder and president of the Earth Policy Institute, a nonprofit think tank. He is also the author of numerous books.

In 1991, a national wind resource inventory taken by the U.S. Department of Energy startled the world when it reported that the three most wind-rich states—North Dakota, Kansas, and Texas—had enough harnessable wind energy to satisfy national electricity needs. Now a new study by a team of engineers at Stanford reports that the wind energy potential is actually substantially greater than that estimated in 1991.

Lester R. Brown, "Wind Power Set to Become the World's Leading Energy Source," www.earth-policy.org, January 25, 2003. Copyright © 2003 Earth Policy Institute. Reproduced by permission.

Advances in wind turbine design since 1991 allow turbines to operate at lower wind speeds, to harness more of the wind's energy, and to harvest it at greater heights—dramatically expanding the harnessable wind resource. Add to this the recent bullish assessments of offshore wind potential, and the enormity of the wind resource becomes apparent. Wind power can meet not only all U.S. electricity needs, but all U.S. energy needs.

Vast Potential

In a joint assessment of global wind resources called Wind Force 12, the European Wind Energy Association and Greenpeace concluded that the world's wind-generating potential—assuming that only 10 percent of the earth's land area would be available for development—is double the projected world electricity demand in 2020. A far larger share of the land area could be used

Mike Keefe. © 2001 by Denver Post. Reproduced by permission of Cagle Cartoons, Inc.

for wind generation in sparsely populated, wind-rich regions, such as the Great Plains of North America, northwest China, eastern Siberia, and the Patagonian region of Argentina. If the huge off-shore potential is added to this, it seems likely that wind power could satisfy not only world electricity needs but perhaps even total energy needs.

Over the last decade wind has been the world's fastest-growing energy source. Rising from 4,800 megawatts of generating capacity in 1995 to 31,100 megawatts in 2002, it increased a staggering sixfold. Worldwide, wind turbines now supply enough electricity to satisfy the residential needs of 40 million Europeans.

Affordable and Abundant

Wind is popular because it is abundant, cheap, inexhaustible, widely distributed, climate-benign, and clean—attributes that no other energy source can match. The cost of wind-generated electricity has dropped from 38¢ a kilowatt-hour in the early 1980s to roughly 4¢ a kilowatt-hour today on prime wind sites. Some recently signed U.S. and U.K. [United Kingdom] long-term supply contracts are providing electricity at 3¢ a kilowatt-hour. Wind Force 12 projected that the average cost per kilowatt hour of wind-generated electricity will drop to 2.6¢ by 2010 and to 2.1¢ by 2020. U.S. energy consultant Harry Braun says that if wind turbines are mass-produced on assembly lines like automobiles, the cost of wind-generated electricity could drop to 1–2¢ per kilowatt hour.

Although wind-generated electricity is already cheap, its cost continues to fall. In contrast with oil, there is no OPEC [Organization of Petroleum Exporting Countries] to set prices for wind. And in contrast to natural gas prices, which are highly volatile and can double in a matter of months, wind prices are declining.

In wind-rich areas of China, wind farms satisfy a small part of China's energy needs.

Another great appeal of wind is its wide distribution. In the United States, for example, some 28 states now have utility-scale wind farms feeding electricity into the local [power] grid. While a small handful of countries controls the world's oil, nearly all countries can tap wind energy.

European Leaders in Wind Power

Denmark leads the world in the share of its electricity from wind—20 percent. In terms of sheer generating capacity, Germany leads with 12,000 megawatts. By the end of 2003, it will have already surpassed its 2010 goal of 12,500 megawatts of generating capacity. For Germany, this rapid growth in wind power is central to reaching its goal of reducing carbon emissions 40 percent by 2020.

Rapid worldwide growth is projected to continue as more countries turn to wind. In addition to the early leaders—Denmark, Germany, Spain, and the United States—many other countries have ambitious plans, including the United Kingdom, France, Brazil, and China.

In densely populated Europe, the off-shore potential for developing wind is also being exploited. Denmark is now building its second off-shore wind farm, this one with 160 megawatts of generating capacity. Germany has some 12,000 megawatts of off-shore generating capacity under consideration.

Wind Can Make Hydrogen

Wind power is now a viable, robust, fast-growing industry. Cheap electricity from wind makes it economical to electrolyze water and produce hydrogen. Hydrogen is the fuel of choice for the highly efficient fuel cells that will be used widely in the future to power motor vehicles and to supply electricity, heating, and cooling for buildings. Hydrogen also offers a way of storing wind energy and of transporting it efficiently by pipeline or in liquefied form by ship.

With the wind industry's engineering know-how and manufacturing experience, it would be relatively easy to scale up the size of the industry, even doubling it annually for several years, if the need arose. If, for example, crop-shrinking heat waves raise food prices and generate public pressure to quickly reduce carbon emissions by replacing coal and oil with wind and hydrogen, it will be possible to do so. If the need arises to shift quickly to hydrogen-fueled automobiles, this can be done by converting gasoline-burning internal combustion engines to hydrogen with inexpensive conversion kits.

Wind Energy's Future

For energy investors, growth in the future lies with wind and the hydrogen produced with cheap wind-generated electricity.

Solar cell sales are growing at over 30 percent a year and are likely to supply much of the electricity for the 1.7 billion people who are still without electricity, most of them living in developing country villages. But solar cells are still too costly to supply the vast amounts of energy required to power a modern economy.

World coal burning peaked in 1996 and has fallen 2 percent since then. It is a fading industry, not an exciting investment prospect. Nor is oil particularly promising, since world production is not likely to expand far beyond current levels. Production

Workers install a solar energy system in New York. Solar energy is too expensive for large-scale energy use.

of natural gas, the cleanest and least climate-disruptive of the fossil fuels, is likely to continue expanding for a few more decades, fortuitously developing an infrastructure that can be adapted for hydrogen. Nuclear power generation is expected to peak soon, when the large number of aging plants that will be closing down will exceed the small number of plants that are under construction.

The energy future belongs to wind. The world energy economy became progressively more global during the twentieth century as the world turned to oil. It promises to reverse direction and become more local during the twenty-first century as the world turns to wind, wind-generated hydrogen, and solar cells. Wind and wind-generated hydrogen will shape not only the energy sector of the global economy but the global economy itself.

Wind Power May Drive the Hydrogen Fuel Revolution

Dawn Levy

Today, wind energy is most often used to generate electricity for use in homes and businesses. In the following selection Dawn Levy describes plans to use wind power to produce hydrogen as a fuel for motor vehicles. Stanford University researchers, she writes, have found that converting all gasoline-powered vehicles to hydrogen-powered ones would have profound benefits, provided that the hydrogen is obtained from a nonpolluting source. Such a conversion would greatly reduce the production of greenhouse gases, which many scientists believe cause global warming. Wind energy, the researchers state, is the most promising way to produce hydrogen because it is nonpolluting. The researchers also claim that the costs of wind-produced hydrogen will compare favorably to the costs associated with producing fossil fuels. Dawn Levy is a science writer for the Stanford University News Service. A 1991 graduate of Columbia University's Graduate School of Journalism, she is a member of the Northern California Science Writers Association.

What if all the vehicles now on the road in the United States were suddenly powered by hydrogen fuel cells? Stanford [University] researchers say in a June 24 [2005] article in the journal *Science* that such a conversion would improve air quality, health and climate—especially if wind were used to generate the electricity needed to split water and make hydrogen in a pollutionless process.

Similarly to how gas is pumped into tanks, hydrogen would be pumped into fuel cells, which rely on chemistry, not combustion, to power vehicles. (As hydrogen flows through fuel-cell compartments, it reacts with oxygen to produce water and energy.) Associate Professor Mark Z. Jacobson and postdoctoral fellow Whitney Goldsborough Colella (both in the Civil and Environmental Engineering Department) and Consulting Professor David M. Golden (Mechanical Engineering Department) report that annually such a conversion could prevent millions of cases of respiratory illness and tens of thousands of hospitalizations and save more lives than were lost in the [September 11, 2001] World Trade Center attacks.

"Converting all the current vehicles to fuel-cell vehicles powered by wind would save 3,000 to 6,000 lives in the United States annually, and it could be done at a fuel cost that's comparable to the cost of gasoline, and less than the cost of gasoline when you consider the health effects of gasoline," said Jacobson, who has no financial interest in any wind or hydrogen endeavor but whose commitment to clean air is manifest in his choice of car (a Toyota Prius [hybrid]), house (it's solar-powered) and career (atmospheric scientist).

Sponsored by the Global Climate and Energy Project at Stanford and by NASA [National Aeronautics and Space Administration], the *Science* study compared emissions that would be produced in five cases—if all vehicles on the road were powered by 1) conventional internal-combustion engines; 2) a combination of electricity and internal combustion of gasoline, as in hybrid vehicles; 3) hydrogen generated from wind electrolysis; 4) hydrogen generated from natural gas; and 5) hydrogen generated from coal gasification.

Hydrogen from Wind

Wind is the most promising means of generating hydrogen, said Jacobson, who with former postdoctoral fellow Cristina Archer recently published a study that mapped global winds and

Hydrogen-fueled vehicles might decrease air pollution but they would not solve the problem of congestion on a Canadian highway.

showed [that] the world, especially the United States, has more than enough wind to meet all its energy needs. Jacobson envisions wind turbines generating electricity on wind farms that are linked in a network to ensure energy production even when parts of the [power] grid have windless days. The electricity would travel through transmission lines to a filling station—similar to today's gas stations. There, it would enter an electrolyzer, which applies the current to water and splits it into oxygen and hydrogen, which are then separated. The hydrogen is then compressed and stored.

A lot of hydrogen is currently produced by another method Jacobson's group analyzed: steam reforming of natural gas. If you take methane, the main component of natural gas, and expose it to steam, the final products are primarily carbon dioxide and hydrogen. While the production of carbon dioxide, a greenhouse gas, is undesirable, the process produces about 55 percent less carbon dioxide than does internal combustion, Jacobson said. Other pollutants result as well, such as oxides of nitrogen and carbon monoxide, but these are still far lower than emissions from gasoline combustion. Steam reformers could be placed at individual filling stations, and methane could be piped in through existing natural gas lines. But natural gas supplies are limited and subject to price fluctuations that hurt the long-term feasibility of this option.

The third hydrogen production method the researchers analyzed is coal gasification, in which hydrogen could be produced at centralized plants, compressed and most likely transported in trucks. Coal is mostly carbon, but also contains hydrogen and sulfur. Exposed to water at high temperature and high pressure, it chemically reacts to yield carbon monoxide and hydrogen. Oxygen from additional water vapor turns carbon monoxide into carbon dioxide. So the end products are primarily carbon dioxide and hydrogen gas. Since coal contains more carbon per unit of energy than does natural gas, making a given amount of hydrogen from coal produces a lot more carbon dioxide than does making it from natural gas.

Hybrid vehicles were better at reducing carbon dioxide than vehicles using hydrogen from coal gasification, Jacobson said. But health costs were lower with coal gasification compared with hybrids, which produce more pollutants since they employ a combustion process.

Toward a Hydrogen Economy

"Switching from a fossil-fuel economy to a hydrogen economy would be subject to technological hurdles, the difficulty of creating a new energy infrastructure and considerable conversion costs but could provide health, environmental, climate and

A hydrogen fuel cell bus in Australia is part of an experiment on hydrogen-fueled public transportation.

economic benefits and reduce the reliance on diminishing oil supplies," the Stanford authors wrote.

While envisioning such a switch may seem like a purely academic exercise, it's not. Such exercises inform policy—albeit sometimes too late. Currently, Congress is debating an energy bill that contains a $4,000 tax credit for diesel vehicles—the same break hybrid vehicles get—because of their perceived higher mileage compared to gasoline vehicles. But a study led by Jacobson and published in 2004 by *Geophysical Review Letters* showed that converting the U.S. vehicle fleet from gasoline to diesel vehicles—even with advanced emissions and particle control technologies—would actually increase photochemical smog, particularly in the Southeastern United States. The reason is that even advanced diesel vehicles may emit more oxides of nitrogen than do gasoline-powered vehicles, and these oxides spur ozone production. Jacobson believes such a tax break may provide an unintentional incentive to damage people's health.

Computer simulations that model the effects of future vehicle fleets may help society assess its best energy options. "Going down the hydrogen pathway is a good thing overall and it's a practical thing, and it's going to be beneficial in terms of air pollution and climate and health," Jacobson said.

California's Contribution

The hydrogen economy is on the horizon. California already has several hydrogen filling stations, and Gov. Arnold Schwarzenegger has proposed an ambitious network of hydrogen filling stations by 2010. Most car manufacturers have prototype hydrogen fuel-cell vehicles. California even has a test fleet of hydrogen buses.

While some are concerned about hydrogen's explosiveness, Jacobson said another property of hydrogen—its lightness—may lessen this danger. He cited an example of two cars—one conventional, one hydrogen-powered—that were hit from behind. The car powered by an internal combustion engine became engulfed in flames when its gas tank was punctured. But when the hydrogen car's fuel cell was punctured, since hydrogen is 14 times lighter than air, the flames just shot straight up. The car was saved.

California governor Arnold Schwarzenegger (left) inaugurates the first hydrogen fueling station in Los Angeles in 2004.

Hydrogen's volatility, however, underscores the need to develop tight seals to prevent leakage from storage tanks, filling stations and the fuel cells themselves.

Cheaper than Gasoline

Because wind generation of hydrogen provided the best health and climate benefits, the researchers did a cost analysis to compare the cost of a gallon of gasoline with that of a gallon of hydrogen generated by wind electrolysis. The cost of making hydrogen from wind is $1.12 to $3.20 per gallon of gasoline or diesel equivalent ($3 to $7.40 per kilogram of molecular hydrogen)—on [a] par with the current price of gas. But gasoline has a hidden cost of 29 cents to $1.80 per gallon in societal costs such as reduced health, lost productivity, hospitalization and death, as well as cleanup of polluted sites. So gasoline's true cost in March 2005, for example, was $2.35 to $3.99 per gallon, which exceeds the estimated mean cost of hydrogen from wind ($2.16 equivalent per gallon of gasoline).

The Stanford study, unprecedented in its detail, used an inventory of more than 600,000 pollution sources reported by the U.S. Environmental Protection Agency (EPA) from August 1999. Colella altered the EPA emission inventory in response to each of the different scenarios. Her work led to a separate paper as well, now in press at the *Journal of Power Sources*. Golden contributed expertise in atmospheric chemistry, and Jacobson plugged Colella's new emission scenarios into his own computer model to run simulations and analyze the resulting costs and effects.

"We believe the results are conservative since health costs associated mostly with particles are now thought to be greater than those used in our study," Jacobson said. "In addition, in the future we will have more fossil [fuel] vehicles than we currently have. So the future health benefit of switching will be greater than in our current study, which assumes an instantaneous switch."

But no matter how many vehicles are on the road, fuel-cell vehicles using hydrogen from wind are not going to produce any real pollution, he emphasized.

"Hybrids are a stepping stone, but they can't be the final destination because even though they result in an improved efficiency over the current vehicle fleet, their numbers will increase," Jacobson said. "Carbon dioxide and other pollutant emissions associated with hybrids will increase as well. So this is not a viable, long-term solution in the presence of a growing population and the desire of many developing countries to industrialize."

Next the group plans to look at the effects of converting all power plants to hydrogen fuel-cell power plants. They also plan to explore the long-term effects of switching to a hydrogen economy on global climate change and the ozone layer.

How to Encourage Investment in Wind and Hydrogen

Jacobson advocates an "Apollo Program"[1] for generating electricity from wind and producing hydrogen using wind-generated

1. The 1960s project to land an astronaut on the Moon.

electricity. Such a program would involve fossil sources paying their true health and climate costs. For example, some old coal-fired plants are exempt from modern performance standards required by Clean Air Act amendments and therefore run inexpensively while saddling society with huge hidden costs. An Apollo Program would provide additional subsidies for wind and other renewable energy sources. While wind subsidies are on the order of $100 million per year, Jacobson said, other energy sources hog subsidies of $15 billion to $20 billion. He advocates supporting the infrastructure needed for wind production of hydrogen to a level similar to the $20 billion recently proposed for a new natural gas pipeline from the continental United States to Alaska.

"If you want to encourage hydrogen and [wind-produced] hydrogen, then you do need to undertake an Apollo Program, because even though the cost of a new wind turbine averaged over a long time is similar to a new coal or natural gas power plant, there's no incentive to replace these other sources with wind."

Facts About Wind

The Nature of Wind

- The uneven heating of Earth's surface by the sun creates wind. Uneven heating produces pressure imbalances. Wind is created when high-pressure air masses rush into low-pressure regions.
- Wind is one of the oldest sources of energy exploited by humankind. Ancient Egyptian records show that wind was used to power sailing vessels on the Nile more than five thousand years ago.
- Wind energy is nonpolluting. It requires no mining, drilling, or transportation of fuel, and it does not generate radioactive or other hazardous waste.
- Wind at useful speeds of 15 miles (24km) per hour or higher exists in every region of the world, but the greatest concentration of land-based wind energy potential is in North America.

How Wind Turbines Work

- Wind energy is typically captured by windmill blades, which convert the lateral force of the wind into a rotary force that can turn an electrical generator or pump water from underground.
- The taller the turbine, the more wind it captures, because winds are usually stronger higher in the atmosphere.
- Wind turbines can be used as stand-alone applications or connected to an electric power grid. Stand-alone turbines are typically used for pumping water or for small-scale electricity generation. Some farmers and homeowners install a single wind turbine to supply them with water or electricity. Large-scale generation typically links large numbers of turbines to a utility grid. When turbines are amassed in this way, they are referred to as wind farms.

Wind Energy Generation

- Wind supplied electric power to more than 1.6 million U.S. households in 2004.
- Wind energy generation capacity grew 35 percent in 2004, as another 2,431 megawatts came online.
- Wind currently supplies less than 1 percent of America's electricity, but it is the fastest-growing source of new electrical power in the United States.
- Wind energy usage in the United States is highest in California. The Golden State leads the nation with the most wind power produced, at 2,150 megawatts. Texas is second, producing 1,995 megawatts.

Glossary

Alternating Current (AC): Electricity that switches direction many times each second. AC allows for transmission over long distances with comparatively little loss in power. (See also Direct Current.)

Alternator: A generator that produces alternating current from the rotation of magnets inside a coil.

Amperage: A measure of electrical current that takes account of the flow rate of electrons through a wire.

Anemometer: A device that measures wind speed. It is typically made from three cups spinning on a vertical axis.

Armature: The moving part of an electrical generator or motor.

Blade: The winglike part of the turbine that engages the wind. Most turbines have either two or three blades.

Controller: Most modern wind turbines have a computer-run controller that shuts off the machine when wind speeds become too high. Excessive speed can burn out the generator.

Cycles per Second: In electricity, the number of times an AC circuit reverses direction.

Direct Current (DC): A type of electric current in which there is a continuous flow of electrons through a conducting material such as a metal wire from an area of negative charge to an area of positive charge.

Dynamo: A rotating generator that produces direct current.

Environmental Impact Statement: A detailed study of the environmental consequences of a proposed electric utility project, such as the erection of a wind turbine.

Fuel Cell: A battery-like piece of equipment used to generate electricity.

Generation: The conversion of other forms of energy into electricity through the use of equipment. Generation is usually measured in kilowatt-hours.

Green Energy: A popular term for energy produced from renewable energy resources. (See also Renewable Energy.)

Hertz: A measure of frequency in AC. (See Cycles per Second.)

Kilowatt: A thousand watts. (See Watt.)

Kilowatt Hour: A unit of energy equal to the work done by a kilowatt over a period of one hour. Often abbreviated as "kwh."

Megawatt: A million watts. (See Watt.)

Nacelle: A streamlined enclosure that sits atop the tower of a wind turbine and protects the gear box, generator, and controller.

Pitch: The twisting of blades to increase or decrease rotor speed in response to changing wind conditions.

Polder Mill: A water-pumping windmill that has been used to reclaim low-lying land vulnerable to flooding, especially in the Netherlands.

Post Mill: A medieval windmill in which the entire building had to be turned around a central post to align the rotor with the wind. (See also Smock Mill.)

Renewable Energy: Energy derived from resources that are naturally regenerated, such as flowing water or wind.

Rotor: The blades and hub of a wind turbine.

Smock Mill: A medieval windmill whose cap rotates to meet the wind while the lower part of the building remains fixed. (See also Post Mill.)

Tower: A tall structure that supports a wind generator. Wind speeds typically rise with height, so the taller the tower, the more efficient the generator.

Transformer: A mechanism that transfers AC current from one circuit to another with a change of voltage in the transfer.

Turbine: A device, such as a windmill, that converts flow into rotation, driving a generator.

Vane: A large, flat extension on the rear of a wind turbine that swings the rotor into the wind.

Variable Pitch: A type of wind turbine rotor where the angle of the blades can be adjusted. (See also Pitch.)

Vertical Axis Wind Turbine: A wind generator in which the rotating shaft stands upright, with blades or cups extending out from it.

Volt: A measure of electrical potential difference. One volt is the potential difference in charge needed to make one Ampere of electrons flow.

Watt: An internationally recognized measure of electrical energy. A typical lightbulb requires 60 watts of electrical power.

Wind Generator: A device that uses the force of the wind to generate electricity. (See also Wind Turbine.)

Windmill: Originally, a device that uses wind power to grind grain into flour, now used to denote any device that puts wind energy to work.

Wind Turbine: A machine that captures the force of the wind to generate electricity. (See also Wind Generator.)

Chronology

ca. 6000 B.C.
The use of sails is first recorded in Egypt. The sails are raised over papyrus rafts that navigate rivers.

ca. 2500
The voyage of a seagoing fleet of wooden sailing vessels is recorded in the tomb of Egyptian pharaoh Sahure.

ca. 650 A.D.
The first windmills begin to appear in Persia, near the border between modern-day Iran and Afghanistan.

1180
Documents record the first known instance of a windmill in Europe, sited near Normandy, France.

1219
The use of vertical-axis windmills in China is recorded by the Chinese statesman Yehlu Chu-Tsai.

1270
The first illustrations of a European windmill appear. They show a relatively sophisticated four-bladed horizontal rotor connected to wooden gears that translate the motion of the blades to a central post.

ca. 1500
The Dutch begin to use windmills, called polders, to drain low-lying land of water. Eventually, the polder mills recover much of the territory of the Netherlands from below sea level.

1605
Spanish author Miguel de Cervantes publishes the novel *Don Quixote*, in which the title character mistakes windmills for dragons.

1854
Connecticut mechanic Daniel Halladay invents a self-regulating windmill to pump water from the ground.

1857
James Mitchell of Woodsfield, Ohio, patents an improved self-governing windmill. It becomes widely used.

1888
Charles Francis Brush, founder of General Electric, builds the first windmill used to generate electricity. It is erected behind his mansion in Cleveland, Ohio.

1891
In Denmark, inventor Poul La Cour designs a high-speed wind turbine for generating electricity.

ca. 1925
Small wind turbines begin to dot the rural landscape of the United States, providing electricity to farms for the first time.

1931
Soviet engineers build the first large-scale wind turbine on the shores of the Caspian Sea. The generator is capable of cranking out one hundred kilowatts.

1941
The first megawatt-class wind turbine is erected on a mountain-top in Vermont. The Smith-Putnam turbine generates up to 1.25 megawatts of power, but its rotor snaps after just four years of service.

1957
Danish engineer Johannes Juul designs the first three-bladed wind turbine. He also creates the first alternating current wind generator.

ca. 1960
German scientist Ulrich Hutter develops revolutionary new wind turbines made from fiberglass and other lightweight materials, with rotors that tilt in high winds to shed excessive loads of wind.

1973
The first oil embargo, led by Middle East nations, prompts the U.S. government to renew federal research into wind energy for the first time since World War II. Work begins on what will soon

become America's first commercial wind farm, at Altamont Pass in northern California.

1975
The National Aeronautics and Space Administration (NASA) begins building large wind turbines at its facilities. Though flawed, they blaze a trail for later American developments in large-scale wind generators.

1976
Federal researchers develop new small-scale wind turbines capable of generating enough electricity for a household. They are later distributed to commercial manufacturers who market them.

1985
A drop in petroleum prices causes interest in wind energy development to flag. Although some countries, such as Denmark, continue to forge ahead, innovation and expansion in wind energy stall in the United States.

2001
Petroleum prices begin to rise as predictions of the end of oil emerge, kindling renewed interest in renewable energy sources.

2004
The Center for Biological Diversity files suit against the owners of the Altamont Pass wind farm in northern California, arguing that the wind turbines kill large numbers of birds. Denmark establishes the goal that it will use wind to generate 20 percent of its electricity.

2005
Debate erupts in Nantucket over plans for the nation's first offshore wind farm. The farm would contain more than a hundred wind turbines rooted in the shallow waters off the Massachusetts shoreline. Opponents claim it would destroy the natural beauty and ecological integrity of the area. Meanwhile, America's wind generators churn out twenty-five hundred megawatts of electric power, enough to supply the needs of half a million homes. While this is only a tiny fraction of the nation's electric supply, industry officials predict the share will grow to 6 percent by 2020.

For Further Reading

Books

Asmus, Peter, *Reaping the Wind: How Mechanical Wizards, Visionaries, and Profiteers Helped Shape Our Energy Future.* Washington, DC: Island Press, 2001.

Baker, T. Lindsay, *A Field Guide to American Windmills.* Norman: University of Oklahoma Press, 1985.

Brower, M.S., et al., *Powering the Midwest: Renewable Electricity for the Economy and the Environment.* Cambridge, MA: Union of Concerned Scientists, 1993.

Gipe, Paul, *Wind Power: Renewable Energy for Home, Farm, and Business.* White River Junction, VT: Chelsea Green, 2004.

Hansen, Martin O.L., *Aerodynamics of Wind Turbines, Rotors, Loads, and Structure.* London: James & James, 2000.

Koeppl, G.W., *Putnam's Power from the Wind*, 2nd ed. New York: Van Nostrand Reinhold, 1982.

Righter, Robert W., *Wind Energy in America: A History.* Norman: University of Oklahoma Press, 1996.

Spera, David A., *Wind Turbine Technology: Fundamental Concepts of Wind Turbine Engineering.* Fairfield, NJ: American Society of Mechanical Engineers, 1994.

Tecco, Betsy Dru, *Wind Power of the Future: New Ways of Turning Wind into Energy.* New York: Rosen, 2003.

Periodicals

Associated Press, "Some Officials Fear Wind 'Ghost Farms,'" January 1, 2006. www.grandforks.com.

Associated Press, "Store Wind Power for Later Use? Cities Bet on It," January 4, 2006. http://msnbc.msn.com.

Boston Globe, "Sneak Attack on Wind Farm," December 17, 2005. www.boston.com.

Buncombe, Andrew, "How the Wind Could Be Our Best Weapon Against Global Warming," *Independent*, December 6, 2005. http://news.independent.co.uk.

Christoffersen, John, "Debate Swirls as Wind Power Grows Rapidly," Associated Press, January 1, 2006. www.boston.com.

Dean, Cornelia, "Congress May Block Plan for a Wind Farm in Nantucket Sound," *New York Times*, December 15, 2005.

Elliott, Valerie, "Wind Farms Condemned as Eagles Fall Prey to Turbines," *Times*, January 28, 2006. www.timesonline.co.uk.

Johnson, G.D., et al., "Collision Mortality of Local and Migrant Birds at a Large-Scale Wind-Power Development on Buffalo Ridge, Minnesota," *Wildlife Society Bulletin*, Fall 2002.

Kueppers, Alfred, "Siemens Invests More than 50 Million Euro to Expand Wind Power Production," *AFX News*, February 2, 2006. www.forbes.com.

National Wind Coordinating Committee, "Avian/Wind Turbine Interaction: A Short Summary of Research Results and Remaining Questions," 2002. www.nationalwind.org.

New Energy Report, "Altamont Wind Farm Will Shut Down Half of Its Turbines," November 27, 2005. www.newenergyreport.org.

Oil & Gas Journal, "Wind Power Capacity Added in '05 Sets Record," February 2, 2006.

Quinn, Steve, "Wind Power Huffs and Puffs Up 35 Percent Gain," Associated Press, January 24, 2006. www.chron.com.

Ritter, John, "Wind Turbines Taking Toll on Birds of Prey," *USA Today*, January 4, 2005. www.usatoday.com.

Williams, Wendy, "When Blade Meets Bat: Unexpected Bat Kills Threaten Future Wind Farms," *Scientific American*, February 2004.

Web Sites

American Wind Energy Association (www.awea.org). The American Wind Energy Association is a national trade association that represents wind power plant developers, wind turbine manufacturers, utilities, consultants, insurers, financiers, researchers, and others involved in the wind industry. Its Web site offers up-to-date news about wind energy development, advocacy for the industry, and statistical information.

British Wind Energy Association (www.bwea.com). The British Wind Energy Association is the trade and professional body for the United Kingdom's wind and marine renewable energy industries. With over 310 corporate members, BWEA takes an active interest in all issues affecting the industry, from financing and planning to political engagement. Its Website includes annual reports and statistics.

Center for Biological Diversity (www.biologicaldiversity.org). This nonprofit wildlife advocacy organization has taken the lead in fighting to reduce bird deaths caused by thousands of wind turbines sited in Altamont Pass, California. The center's Web site includes information about the center's position on making wind energy safe and its lawsuit against the owners of the Altamont Pass wind farm.

Danish Wind Industry Association (www.windpower.org). The Danish Wind Industry Association Web site has English-language pages that provide news and information about wind power development in the world's leading wind-energy nation.

National Renewable Energy Laboratory (www.nrel.gov). The National Renewable Energy Laboratory is the U.S. Department of Energy's key program to secure an environmentally and economically sustainable energy future for the nation. Its Web site includes a section on the laboratory's National Wind Technology Center.

National Wind Coordinating Committee (www.nationalwind.org). A U.S.-based collaborative formed in 1994, the National Wind Coordinating Committee (NWCC) identifies and analyzes issues that affect the use of wind power in order to support the development of environmentally, economically, and politically sustainable commercial markets for wind power. NWCC members include representatives from private and public stakeholders. The NWCC Web site contains numerous policy papers and issue analyses.

Office of Energy Efficiency and Renewable Energy (www.eere. energy.gov). The Office of Energy Efficiency and Renewable Energy, a division of the U.S. Department of Energy, promotes public awareness about energy efficiency and renewable energy sources. Its Web site includes extensive information about wind energy technologies and applications.

Sandia National Laboratories (www.sandia.gov). The Sandia National Laboratories, a government-owned, privately operated set of facilities, conducts applied wind energy research to improve wind turbine performance and reduce cost. The program is divided into three major programmatic areas: low wind speed technology, supporting research and technology, and technology applications. The Sandia Web site includes extensive archives of research reports.

Windustry (www.windustry.org). Windustry is a nonprofit organization working to promote wind energy opportunities for rural communities. It establishes collaborations with rural landowners, local communities, and utilities, as well as state, regional, and nonprofit organizations, primarily in the Midwest.

Index

Advanced Energy Initiative (AEI), 10
Altamont Pass Wind Resource Area (APWRA), bird kills at, 14–16, 46–47, 50
  as atypical, 57–59
American Wind Energy Association (AWEA), 12
Archer, Christina, 103
Australian Wind Energy Association, 47

Baker, T. Lindsay, 33
Beedell, Suzanne, 24
birds
  leading cause of deaths to cats, 57
  collisions, 54–55
  electrical lines, 53
  pesticides, 57
  wind farms as danger to, 14–15, 65
  as insignificant, 57–61
  other causes vs., 56
Block, Leo, 20
Braun, Harry, 97
Brown, Lester R., 10, 95
Brunell, Don, 93
Burrington, Stephen, 97
Bush, George W., 10

Cape Cod National Seashore, 66

Cape Wind, 64, 66, 68, 69
Center for Biological Diversity, 15
Chapman, Andrew, 45
coal
  decline in use, 100
  gasification, in production of hydrogen, 105–106
Colella, Whitney Goldsborough, 103, 109
Competitive Enterprise Institute, 89
Crowley, Carolyn, 43
Crowley, Claude, 43

Denmark, wind energy and, 80, 98
Department of Energy, U.S. (DOE), 10
  on deepwater wind farms, 77
  on potential of wind energy, 95
Dunlop, John, 79

Eaglehawk Conservation Group (Australia), 49
edge mills, 29
Egyptians, use of sailing craft, 20–23
electricity, wind-generated cost of, 97
  in megawatts, by state, 84
Environmental Protection Agency (EPA), 109

Europe
  energy is more expensive in, 93–94
  wind power in, 80
    increase in, 97
    potential of, 99
European Wind Energy Association, 96
Evans, William, 60
Exley, Peter, 47
Exxon Valdez oil spill (1989), 55

Flatow, Ira, 79

Geophysical Review Letters (journal), 107
Germany, wind energy in, 98–99
Gillespie, W.P., 40
Global Climate and Energy Project (Stanford University), 103
Golden, David M., 103, 109
Greenpeace, 96

Halladay, Daniel, 36–37
Howe, Robert, 59
Hrab, Neil, 89
Humane Society, 65
hydrogen
  switch to economy based on, 106–107
  vehicles, 102–103
  wind power in production of, 99, 103, 105
  cost of, 108

International Federation of Industrial Energy Consumers (IFIEC), 93–94

Jacobson, Mark Z., 103, 105, 106, 109
Journal of Power Resources, 109

Kennedy, Robert F., Jr., 63, 69
Kreuger, Max, 35–36

Levy, Dawn, 102

Miller, Jeff, 49
Mitchell, James, 37

Nantucket wind farm
  as blight on landscape, 65–67
  con, 73
  environmental hazards of, 65
  opposition to, 17
  would harm local industries, 65–66
  would reduce New England's oil use, 74
Nash, E.D., 37–38
National Renewable Energy Laboratory, 68
Natural Resources Defense Council (NRDC), 77, 92
natural gas, 100–101
  in production of hydrogen, 105
Netherlands
  preservation of windmills in, 32

use of windmills in
  in grinding, 29–30
  in land drainage, 25–28
Nimitz, Charles H., 40–41
nuclear power, 101

oil, decline in production of,
  10, 100
oil mills, 29–30

polder mills, 27–29

Royal Society for the
  Protection of Birds, U.K.
  (RSPB), 47–48

Sagrillo, Mick, 52
sailing craft, Egyptian,
  20–23
saw mills, 30–32
Schwarzenegger, Arnold,
  107
Science (journal), 102
Sierra Club, 13, 91–92
Sloan, Mike, 79
solar energy
  growth in, 100
  is preferable to wind energy,
  51
Starfish Hill windfarm, 49
subsidies
  are needed for wind power,
  110
  pro-wind lobbyists seek,
  90–92
  for wind power in Europe,
  93–94
Swisher, Randall, 14

Talk of the Nation: Science
  Friday (radio program), 79
Texas
  windmills in, 35–39
    for access to underground
    water, 40–42
    current use of, 43
    mass production of, 39
  wind power in, 82–84,
    87–88

vehicles, hydrogen-fueled
  benefits of, 102–103
  danger of explosion in, 107
voyages, by sailing craft, 23

wind farms
  as blight on landscape,
    16–17
  as danger to birds, 45–51,
    65
    is insignificant, 57–61
  deepwater, 72–73, 77
Wind Force 12, 96
windmills
  in the Netherlands
    in grinding, 29–30
    in land drainage, 25–28
    preservation of, 32
  in Texas, 35–39
    for access to underground
    water, 40–42
    current use of, 43
    mass production of, 39
wind power
  advantages of, 10–14
  companies stand to profit
    from, 92–93

deepwater technology and, 67–68

disadvantages of, 14–17

electricity generated by
in megawatts, by state, 84
potential, 81–82, 96–97

history of, 34–35
in the Netherlands, 24–32
in sailing craft, 20–23

hydrogen production by, 99, 103, 105
cost of, 108

in Minnesota, 85–86

states leading in, 80

in Texas, 82–84, 87–88

wind turbines
advances in design of, 96
amount paid to ranchers for, 84–85
cost of, 82
parts of, 13
size of, 86

Winkleman, J.E., 47

wip mills, 26–27

Wolf, Amy, 59

Yandle, Bruce, 90

Zervos, Arthourus, 70

Picture Credits

Cover photo: © Lester Lefkowitz/CORBIS
© Anthony West/CORBIS, 78
AP/Wide World Photos, 16, 42, 71, 75
© Archivo Inconografico, S.A./CORBIS, 22
© The Art Archive/CORBIS, 28
© Bob Sacha/CORBIS, 67, 98
© Bruce Murphy/Landov, 108
© Chris Daniels/CORBIS, 44
© Christian Charisius/Reuters/CORBIS, 12
© Danny Lehman/CORBIS, 37
© David T. Grewcock; Frank Lane Picture Agency/
  CORBIS, 58
© Gerald French/CORBIS, 34-35
© Getty Images, 100, 106
© Joseph Paris, 15, 61
© Joson/zefa/CORBIS, 11
© Keren Su/CORBIS, 26
© Lake County Museum/CORBIS, 90
© Layne Kennedy/CORBIS, 80, 86
Library of Congress, 19, 31
© Mike Maass, 54 (main)
© Morton Beebe/CORBIS, 46 (main)
© 1996 CORBIS, 64
© Phil Noble/CORBIS, 76
© PHOTOPRO/Landov, 91
Photos.com, 41, 46 (inset), 50, 54 (inset), 83, 87, 104
© Ric Ergenbright/CORBIS, 30
© Richard Cummins/CORBIS, 38
Victor Habbick Visions, 13, 27, 56, 68, 72, 84
© Waltraud Grubitzsch/dpa/CORBIS, 92

About the Editor

Clay Farris Naff is a journalist, author, and nonprofit executive. He served as a UPI correspondent in Tokyo and later wrote a book on contemporary social change in Japan, published in 1994 by Kodansha International. After resettling in the United States, he published widely on science and religion and edited numerous Greenhaven Press titles on science and medical topics. He serves as executive director of the Lincoln Literacy Council in Lincoln, Nebraska.